Poems Of Today: An Anthology

English Association

Poems of To-Day:

an Anthology.

London:
Published for the English Association
by Sidgwick & Jackson, Ltd., 1915

First issued in August, 1915
Reprinted October, 1915

Printed by Hazell, Watson & Viney, Ld., London and Aylesbury.

THE ENGLISH ASSOCIATION

President, 1915: W. P. KER, LL.D.
Chairman of Committee: JOHN BUCHAN

The aims of the Association are :—

(*a*) To promote the due recognition of English as an essential element in the national education.

(*b*) To discuss methods of teaching English and the correlation of School and University work.

(*c*) To encourage and facilitate advanced study in English literature and language.

(*d*) To unite all those who are interested in English studies; to bring teachers into contact with one another and with writers and readers who do not teach ; and to induce those who are not themselves engaged in teaching to use their influence in the cause of English as a part of education.

The Association should therefore appeal

(*a*) To every one concerned, whether as teacher, examiner, or inspector, .with the teaching of English as an element in University, Secondary, or Primary Education.

(*b*) To persons engaged in literary work.

(*c*) To persons interested in the study of English literature or of the English language, or in the improvement of education in these subjects.

The Association and its local Branches hold meetings during the year, at which lectures are given, or papers are read, or discussions are carried on.

The Association issues yearly three or more Pamphlets on literary subjects and matters connected with the teaching of English, and three Bulletins containing bibliographies of new publications, together with a report of meetings held, and other information likely to be of interest to members. These publications are issued gratis to members.

The ordinary subscription is 5*s.* a year, and the fee for life membership £3 3*s.* Full information will be given to intending members by the Secretary, Imperial College Union, Prince Consort Road, South Kensington, S.W.

PREFATORY NOTE

THIS book has been compiled in order that boys and girls, already perhaps familiar with the great classics of the English speech, may also know something of the newer poetry of their own day. Most of the writers are living, and the rest are still vivid memories among us, while one of the youngest, almost as these words are written, has gone singing to lay down his life for his country's cause. Although no definite chronological limit has been set, and Meredith at least began to write in the middle of the nineteenth century, the intention has been to represent mainly those poetic tendencies which have become dominant as the influence of the accepted Victorian masters has grown weaker, and from which the poetry of the future, however it may develope, must in turn take its start. It may be helpful briefly to indicate the sequence of themes. Man draws his being from the heroic Past and from the Earth his Mother ; and in harmony with these he must shape his life to what high purposes he may. Therefore this gathering of poems falls into three groups.

First there are poems of History, of the romantic tale of the world, of our own special tradition here in England, and of the inheritance of obligation which that tradition imposes upon us. Naturally, there are some poems directly inspired by the present war, but nothing, it is hoped, which may not, in happier days, bear translation into any European tongue. Then there come poems of the Earth, of England again and the longing of the exile for home, of this and that familiar countryside, of woodland and meadow and garden, of the process of the seasons, of the " open road " and the " wind on the heath," of the city, its deprivations and its consolations. Finally there are poems of Life itself, of the moods in which it may be faced, of religion, of man's excellent virtues, of friendship and childhood, of passion, grief, and comfort. But there is no arbitrary isolation of one theme from another ; they mingle and inter-penetrate throughout, to the music of Pan's flute, and of Love's viol, and the bugle-call of Endeavour, and the passing-bell of Death.

May, 1915.

INDEX OF AUTHORS

For permission to use copyright poems the English Association is greatly indebted to the authors; to the literary executors of Mary Coleridge (Sir Henry Newbolt), J. E. Flecker (Mrs. Flecker), Lionel Johnson (Mr. Elkin Mathews), George Meredith (Trustees, through Mr. W. M. Meredith), R. L. Stevenson (Mr. Lloyd Osbourne), Arthur Symons (through Mr. Edmund Gosse), and Francis Thompson (Mr. Wilfrid Meynell); and to the following publishers in respect of the poems enumerated:

Mr. B. H. Blackwell :

A. S. Cripps, *Lyra Evangelistica* (Nos. 25, 26, 39).

Messrs. W. Blackwood & Sons :

Alfred Noyes, *Drake* (No. 12).

Mr. A. H. Bullen :

W. B. Yeats, *Poems* (Nos. 101, 133, 146).

Messrs. Burns & Oates :

Francis Thompson, *Works* (Nos. 105, 106, 110, 123, 127, 145).
Alice Meynell, *Collected Poems* (Nos. 62, 74, 81, 107, 111, 115, 137, 140, 147).
Shane Leslie, *Eyes of Youth* (No. 84).

Messrs. Chatto & Windus :

R. L. Stevenson, *Underwoods* (Nos. 51, 73, 90, 109), and *Songs of Travel* (Nos. 29, 32, 68, 71, 94, 96, 135).

Messrs. Constable & Co. :

Walter de la Mare, *The Listeners* (Nos. 1, 61, 67, 117, 142).

Messrs. J. M. Dent & Sons, Ltd.:
  W. Canton, *The Comrades* (No. 28).
  G. K. Chesterton, *The Wild Knight* (No. 131).

Messrs. Duckworth & Co.:
  Hilaire Belloc, *Verses* (Nos. 35, 45, 112).
  T. Sturge Moore, *The Gazelles* (Nos. 89, 93).

Mr. A. C. Fifield:
  W. H. Davies, *Songs of Joy* (Nos. 48, 86), and
          Nature Poems (No. 53).

Messrs. Max Goschen, Ltd.:
  J. E. Flecker, *The Golden Journey to Samarcand* * (Nos. 24, 60).

Mr. William Heinemann:
  W. S. Blunt, *Poetry of* (Nos. 36, 64, 65).
  Edmund Gosse, *Collected Poems* (Nos. 82, 87).
  Arthur Symons, *Poems* (Nos. 85, 113, 130).

Mr. John Lane:
  L. Abercrombie, *Interludes and Poems* (No. 31).
  John Davidson, *Ballads and Songs* (Nos. 37, 38, 80).
  William Watson, *The Hope of the World* (Nos. 66, 121).
  Margaret L. Woods, *Lyrics and Ballads* (Nos. 10, 91).

Mr. Elkin Mathews:
  Laurence Binyon, *Poems* (1894), (No. 79),
          London Visions (Nos. 75, 77), and
          England (Nos. 16, 57, 129).
  Lionel Johnson, *Poems* (Nos. 9, 95, 118).

Messrs. Maunsel & Co.:
  P. R. Chalmers, *Green Days and Blue Days* (No. 99).
  Padraic Colum, *Wild Earth* (No. 124).

Messrs. Methuen & Co.:
  Rudyard Kipling, *The Seven Seas* (No. 50), and
          The Five Nations (No. 34).
  Sir A. T. Quiller-Couch, *Poems and Ballads* (No. 8), and
          The Vigil of Venus (No. 44).
  Herbert Trench, *New Poems* (Nos. 14, 92).

          * Now transferred to Mr. Martin Secker.

Messrs. Sidgwick & Jackson, Ltd. :
   Rupert Brooke, 1914 *and Other Poems* (Nos. 20, 21, 47).
   John Drinkwater, *Swords and Ploughshares* (Nos. 19, 40, 41).
   Laurence Housman, *Selected Poems* (No. 83).
   Rose Macaulay, *The Two Blind Countries* (No. 46).

Messrs. Smith, Elder & Co. :
   Robert Bridges, *Poetical Works* (Nos. 54, 56, 63, 76, 104, 125,
      126, 128, 132, 139, 141).

Messrs. T. Fisher Unwin, Ltd. :
   Ernest Radford, *Poems* (No. 42).
   W. B. Yeats, *Poems* (Nos. 49, 88, 138, 143, 144).

The Poetry Book Shop (through Mr. Harold Monro).
   Ralph Hodgson, *Eve* (No. 5).

The Editor of *The Times* courteously confirmed the permissions given by Mr. George Russell (" A. E.") in respect of No. 23, and by Mr. Laurence Binyon in respect of No. 22—the latter being reprinted in *The Winnowing Fan* (Elkin Mathews).

The Association desires also to acknowledge the generosity with which authors and publishers have waived or reduced customary copyright fees, in view of the special objects of their organisation. They regret that considerations of copyright have rendered it impossible to include poems by T. E. Brown, Thomas Hardy, W. E. Henley, and A. E. Housman.

POEMS OF TO-DAY

1. ALL THAT'S PAST

VERY old are the woods ;
   And the buds that break
Out of the briar's boughs,
  When March winds wake,
So old with their beauty are—
  Oh, no man knows
Through what wild centuries
  Roves back the rose.

Very old are the brooks ;
  And the rills that rise
Where snow sleeps cold beneath
  The azure skies
Sing such a history
  Of come and gone,
Their every drop is as wise
  As Solomon.

Very old are we men ;
  Our dreams are tales
Told in dim Eden
  By Eve's nightingales ;

I

We wake and whisper awhile,
　　But, the day gone by,
Silence and sleep like fields
　　Of amaranth lie.

Walter de la Mare.

2. PRE-EXISTENCE

I LAID me down upon the shore
　　And dreamed a little space;
I heard the great waves break and roar;
　　The sun was on my face.

My idle hands and fingers brown
　　Played with the pebbles grey;
The waves came up, the waves went down,
　　Most thundering and gay.

The pebbles, they were smooth and round
　　And warm upon my hands,
Like little people I had found
　　Sitting among the sands.

The grains of sands so shining-small
　　Soft through my fingers ran;
The sun shone down upon it all,
　　And so my dream began:

How all of this had been before;
　　How ages far away
I lay on some forgotten shore
　　As here I lie to-day.

The waves came shining up the sands,
   As here to-day they shine ;
And in my pre-pelasgian hands
   The sand was warm and fine.

I have forgotten whence I came,
   Or what my home might be,
Or by what strange and savage name
   I called that thundering sea.

I only know the sun shone down .
   As still it shines to-day,
And in my fingers long and brown
   The little pebbles lay.
Frances Cornford.

3. FRAGMENTS

TROY TOWN is covered up with weeds,
   The rabbits and the pismires brood
On broken gold, and shards, and beads
   Where Priam's ancient palace stood.

The floors of many a gallant house
   Are matted with the roots of grass ;
The glow-worm and the nimble mouse
   Among her ruins flit and pass.

And there, in orts of blackened bone,
   The widowed Trojan beauties lie,
And Simois babbles over stone
   And waps and gurgles to the sky.

Once there were merry days in Troy,
   Her chimneys smoked with cooking meals,
The passing chariots did annoy
   The sunning housewives at their wheels.

And many a lovely Trojan maid
   Set Trojan lads to lovely things ;
The game of life was nobly played,
   They played the game like Queens and Kings.

So that, when Troy had greatly passed
   In one red roaring fiery coal,
The courts the Grecians overcast
   Became a city in the soul.

In some green island of the sea,
   Where now the shadowy coral grows
In pride and pomp and empery
   The courts of old Atlantis rose.

In many a glittering house of glass
   The Atlanteans wandered there ;
The paleness of their faces was
   Like ivory, so pale they were.

And hushed they were, no noise of words
   In those bright cities ever rang ;
Only their thoughts, like golden birds,
   About their chambers thrilled and sang.

They knew all wisdom, for they knew
   The souls of those Egyptian Kings

Who learned, in ancient Babilu,
The beauty of immortal things.

They knew all beauty—when they thought
The air chimed like a stricken lyre,
The elemental birds were wrought,
The golden birds became a fire.

And straight to busy camps and marts
The singing flames were swiftly gone ;
The trembling leaves of human hearts
Hid boughs for them to perch upon.

And men in desert places, men
Abandoned, broken, sick with fears,
Rose singing, swung their swords agen,
And laughed and died among the spears.

The green and greedy seas have drowned
That city's glittering walls and towers,
Her sunken minarets are crowned
With red and russet water-flowers.

In towers and rooms and golden courts
The shadowy coral lifts her sprays ;
The scrawl hath gorged her broken orts,
The shark doth haunt her hidden ways.

But, at the falling of the tide,
The golden birds still sing and gleam,
The Atlanteans have not died,
Immortal things still give us dream.

The dream that fires man's heart to make,
　To build, to do, to sing or say
A beauty Death can never take,
　An Adam from the crumbled clay.

John Masefield.

4. FALLEN CITIES

I GATHERED with a careless hand,
　There where the waters night and day
　Are languid in the idle bay,
A little heap of golden sand;
　And, as I saw it, in my sight
　Awoke a vision brief and bright,
A city in a pleasant land.

I saw no mound of earth, but fair
· Turrets and domes and citadels,
　With murmuring of many bells;
The spires were white in the blue air,
　And men by thousands went and came,
　Rapid and restless, and like flame
Blown by their passions here and there.

With careless hand I swept away
　The little mound before I knew;
　The visioned city vanished too,
And fall'n beneath my fingers lay.
　Ah God! how many hast Thou seen,
　Cities that are not and have been,
By silent hill and idle bay!

Gerald Gould.

5. TIME, YOU OLD GIPSY MAN

TIME, you old gipsy man,
  Will you not stay,
Put up your caravan
  Just for one day ?

All things I'll give you,
Will you be my guest,
Bells for your jennet
Of silver the best,
Goldsmiths shall beat you
A great golden ring,
Peacocks shall bow to you,
Little boys sing,
Oh, and sweet girls will
Festoon you with may,
Time, you old gipsy,
Why hasten away ?

Last week in Babylon,
Last night in Rome,
Morning, and in the crush
Under Paul's dome ;
Under Paul's dial
You tighten your rein—
Only a moment,
And off once again ;
Off to some city
Now blind in the womb,
Off to another
Ere that's in the tomb.

Time, you old gipsy man,
  Will you not stay,
Put up your caravan
  Just for one day ?

                    Ralph Hodgson.

6. A HUGUENOT

O, A gallant set were they,
  As they charged on us that day,
A thousand riding like one !
  Their trumpets crying,
  And their white plumes flying,
And their sabres flashing in the sun.

  O, a sorry lot were we,
    As we stood beside the sea,
Each man for himself as he stood !
    We were scattered and lonely—
    A little force only
Of the good men fighting for the good.

  But I never loved more
    On sea or on shore
The ringing of my own true blade,
    Like lightning it quivered,
    And the hard helms shivered,
As I sang, " None maketh me afraid ! "

                    Mary E. Coleridge.

7. ON THE TOILET TABLE OF QUEEN MARIE-ANTOINETTE

THIS was her table, these her trim outspread
 Brushes and trays and porcelain cups for red ;
Here sate she, while her women tired and curled
The most unhappy head in all the world.

J. B. B. Nichols.

8. UPON ECKINGTON BRIDGE, RIVER AVON

O PASTORAL heart of England ! like a psalm
 Of green days telling with a quiet beat——
O wave into the sunset flowing calm !
 O tirèd lark descending on the wheat !
Lies it all peace beyond that western fold
 Where now the lingering shepherd sees his star
Rise upon Malvern ? Paints an Age of Gold
 Yon cloud with prophecies of linkèd ease——
Lulling this Land, with hills drawn up like knees,
To drowse beside her implements of war ?

Man shall outlast his battles. They have swept
 Avon from Naseby Field to Severn Ham ;
And Evesham's dedicated stones have stepp'd
 Down to the dust with Montfort's oriflamme.
Nor the red tear nor the reflected tower
 Abides ; but yet these eloquent grooves remain,
Worn in the sandstone parapet hour by hour
 By labouring bargemen where they shifted ropes.
 E'en so shall man turn back from violent hopes
To Adam's cheer, and toil with spade again.

Ay, and his mother Nature, to whose lap
   Like a repentant child at length he hies,
Not in the whirlwind or the thunder-clap
   Proclaims her more tremendous mysteries :
But when in winter's grave, bereft of light,
   With still, small voice divinelier whispering
—Lifting the green head of the aconite,
   Feeding with sap of hope the hazel-shoot—
   She feels God's finger active at the root,
Turns in her sleep, and murmurs of the Spring.
Arthur Quiller-Couch.

9. BY THE STATUE OF KING CHARLES AT CHARING CROSS

SOMBRE and rich, the skies ;
   Great glooms, and starry plains.
Gently the night wind sighs ;
Else a vast silence reigns.

The splendid silence clings
Around me : and around
The saddest of all kings
Crowned, and again discrowned.

Comely and calm, he rides
Hard by his own Whitehall :
Only the night wind glides :
No crowds, nor rebels, brawl.

Gone, too, his Court ; and yet,
The stars his courtiers are :
Stars in their stations set ;
And every wandering star.

Alone he rides, alone,
The fair and fatal king :
Dark night is all his own,
That strange and solemn thing.

Which are more full of fate :
The stars ; or those sad eyes ?
Which are more still and great :
Those brows ; or the dark skies ?

Although his whole heart yearn
In passionate tragedy :
Never was face so stern
With sweet austerity.

Vanquished in life, his death
By beauty made amends :
The passing of his breath
Won his defeated ends.

Brief life and hapless ? Nay :
Through death, life grew sublime.
Speak after sentence ?   Yea :
And to the end of time.

Armoured he rides, his head
Bare to the stars of doom :
He triumphs now, the dead,
Beholding London's gloom.

Our wearier spirit faints,
Vexed in the world's employ :

His soul was of the saints ;
And art to him was joy.

King, tried in fires of woe !
Men hunger for thy grace :
And through the night I go,
Loving thy mournful face.

Yet when the city sleeps ;
When all the cries are still :
The stars and heavenly deeps
Work out a perfect will.

Lionel Johnson.

10. TO THE FORGOTTEN DEAD

To the forgotten dead,
        Come, let us drink in silence ere we part.
To every fervent yet resolvèd heart
That brought its tameless passion and its tears,
Renunciation and laborious years,
To lay the deep foundations of our race,
To rear its stately fabric overhead
And light its pinnacles with golden grace.
        To the unhonoured dead.

        To the forgotten dead,
Whose dauntless hands were stretched to grasp the
        rein
Of Fate and hurl into the void again
Her thunder-hoofèd horses, rushing blind
Earthward along the courses of the wind.

Among the stars, along the wind in vain
Their souls were scattered and their blood was shed,
And nothing, nothing of them doth remain.
    To the thrice-perished dead.
Margaret L. Woods.

11. DRAKE'S DRUM

DRAKE he's in his hammock an' a thousand mile
    away,
  (Capten, art tha sleepin' there below ?)
Slung atween the round shot in Nombre Dios Bay,
  An' dreamin' arl the time o' Plymouth Hoe.
Yarnder lumes the Island, yarnder lie the ships,
  Wi' sailor-lads a-dancin' heel-an'-toe,
An' the shore-lights flashin', an' the night-tide dashin',
  He sees et arl so plainly as he saw et long ago.

Drake he was a Devon man, an' rüled the Devon seas,
  (Capten, art tha sleepin' there below ?)
Rovin' tho' his death fell, he went wi' heart at ease,
  An' dreamin' arl the time o' Plymouth Hoe.
" Take my drum to England, hang et by the shore,
  Strike et when your powder's runnin' low ;
If the Dons sight Devon, I'll quit the port o' Heaven,
  An' drum them up the Channel as we drummed
    them long ago."

Drake he's in his hammock till the great Armadas
    come,
  (Capten, art tha sleepin' there below ?)
Slung atween the round shot, listenin' for the drum,
  An' dreamin' arl the time o' Plymouth Hoe.

Call him on the deep sea, call him up the Sound,
   Call him when ye sail to meet the foe ;
Where the old trade's plyin' an' the old flag flyin'
   They shall find him ware an' wakin', as they found
     him long ago !

Henry Newbolt.

12. THE MOON IS UP

THE moon is up : the stars are bright :
   The wind is fresh and free !
We're out to seek for gold to-night
   Across the silver sea !
The world was growing grey and old :
   Break out the sails again !
We're out to seek a Realm of Gold
   Beyond the Spanish Main.

We're sick of all the cringing knees,
   The courtly smiles and lies !
God, let Thy singing Channel breeze
   Lighten our hearts and eyes !
Let love no more be bought and sold
   For earthly loss or gain ;
We're out to seek an Age of Gold
   Beyond the Spanish Main.

Beyond the light of far Cathay,
   Beyond all mortal dreams,
Beyond the reach of night and day
   Our El Dorado gleams,

Revealing—as the skies unfold—
A star without a stain,
The Glory of the Gates of Gold
Beyond the Spanish Main.

Alfred Noyes.

13. MINORA SIDERA

SITTING at times over a hearth that burns
With dull domestic glow,
My thought, leaving the book, gratefully turns
To you who planned it so.

Not of the great only you deigned to tell—
The stars by which we steer—
But lights out of the night that flashed, and fell
To night again, are here.

Such as were those, dogs of an elder day,
Who sacked the golden ports,
And those later who dared grapple their prey
Beneath the harbour forts :

Some with flag at the fore, sweeping the world
To find an equal fight,
And some who joined war to their trade, and hurled
Ships of the line in flight.

Whether their fame centuries long should ring
They cared not over-much,
But cared greatly to serve God and the king,
And keep the Nelson touch ;

And fought to build Britain above the tide
   Of wars and windy fate ;
And passed content, leaving to us the pride
   Of lives obscurely great.

Henry Newbolt.

14. MUSING ON A GREAT SOLDIER

FEAR? Yes . . . I heard you saying
   In an Oxford common-room
Where the hearth-light's kindly raying
Stript the empanelled walls of gloom,
Silver groves of candles playing
In the soft wine turned to bloom—
At the word I see you now
Blandly push the wine-boat's prow
Round the mirror of that scored
Yellow old mahogany board—
I confess to one fear ; this,
To be buried alive !

        My Lord,
Your fancy has played amiss.

Fear not.   When in farewell
While guns toll like a bell
And the bell tolls like a gun
Westminster towers call
Folk and state to your funeral,
And robed in honours won,
Beneath the cloudy pall
Of the lifted shreds of glory

You lie in the last stall
Of that grey dormitory—
Fear not lest mad mischance
Should find you lapt and shrouded
Alive in helpless trance
Though seeming death-beclouded :

For long ere so you rest
On that transcendent bier
Shall we not have addressed
One summons, one last test,
To your reluctant ear ?
O believe it ! we shall have uttered
In ultimate entreaty
A name your soul would hear
Howsoever thickly shuttered ;
We shall have stooped and muttered
England ! in your cold ear. . . .
Then, if your great pulse leap
No more, nor your cheek burn,
Enough ; then shall we learn
'Tis time for us to weep.

Herbert Trench.

15. HE FELL AMONG THIEVES

"YE have robbed," said he, "ye have slaughtered
    and made an end,
Take your ill-got plunder, and bury the dead :
What will ye more of your guest and sometime
    friend ? "
  "Blood for our blood," they said.

2

He laughed: " If one may settle the score for five,
   I am ready ; but let the reckoning stand till day :
I have loved the sunlight as dearly as any alive."
   " You shall die at dawn," said they.

He flung his empty revolver down the slope,
   He climb'd alone to the Eastward edge of the trees ;
All night long in a dream untroubled of hope
   He brooded, clasping his knees.

He did not hear the monotonous roar that fills
   The ravine where the Yassin river sullenly flows ;
He did not see the starlight on the Laspur hills,
   Or the far Afghan snows.

He saw the April noon on his books aglow,
   The wistaria trailing in at the window wide ;
He heard his father's voice from the terrace below
   Calling him down to ride.

He saw the gray little church across the park,
   The mounds that hid the loved and honoured dead ;
The Norman arch, the chancel softly dark,
   The brasses black and red.

He saw the School Close, sunny and green,
   The runner beside him, the stand by the parapet
     wall,
The distant tape, and the crowd roaring between
   His own name over all.

He saw the dark wainscot and timbered roof,
　The long tables, and the faces merry and keen;
The College Eight and their trainer dining aloof,
　The Dons on the daïs serene.

He watch'd the liner's stem ploughing the foam,
　He felt her trembling speed and the thrash of her
　　screw ;
He heard her passengers' voices talking of home,
　He saw the flag she flew.

And now it was dawn.　He rose strong on his feet,
　And strode to his ruin'd camp below the wood ;
He drank the breath of the morning cool and sweet;
　His murderers round him stood.

Light on the Laspur hills was broadening fast,
　The blood-red snow-peaks chilled to a dazzling
　　white ;
He turn'd, and saw the golden circle at last,
　Cut by the eastern height.

" O glorious Life, Who dwellest in earth and sun,
　I have lived, I praise and adore Thee."
　　　　　　　　A sword swept.
Over the pass the voices one by one
　Faded, and the hill slept.

　　　　　　　　　　Henry Newbolt.

16. ENGLAND

SHALL we but turn from braggart pride
    Our race to cheapen and defame ?
Before the world to wail, to chide,
And weakness as with vaunting claim ?
Ere the hour strikes, to abdicate
The steadfast spirit that made us great,
And rail with scolding tongues at fate ?

If England's heritage indeed
Be lost, be traded quite away
For fatted sloth and fevered greed ;
If, inly rotting, we decay ;
Suffer we then what doom we must,
But silent, as befits the dust
Of them whose chastisement was just.

But rather, England, rally thou
Whatever breathes of faith that still
Within thee keeps the undying vow
And dedicates the constant will.
For such yet lives, if not among
The boasters, or the loud of tongue,
Who cry that England's knell is rung.

The faint of heart, the small of brain,
In thee but their own image find :
Beyond such thoughts as these contain
A mightier Presence is enshrined.
Nor meaner than their birthright grown
Shall these thy latest sons be shown,
So thou but use them for thine own.

By those great spirits burning high
In our home's heaven, that shall be stars
To shine, when all is history
And rumour of old, idle wars ;
By all those hearts which proudly bled
To make this rose of England red ;
The living, the triumphant dead ;

By all who suffered and stood fast
That Freedom might the weak uphold,
And in men's ways of wreck and waste
Justice her awful flower unfold ;
By all who out of grief and wrong
In passion's art of noble song
Made Beauty to our speech belong ;

By those adventurous ones who went
Forth overseas, and, self-exiled,
Sought from far isle and continent
Another England in the wild,
For whom no drums beat, yet they fought
Alone, in courage of a thought
Which an unbounded future wrought ;

Yea, and yet more by those to-day
Who toil and serve for naught of gain,
That in thy purer glory they
May melt their ardour and their pain ;
By these and by the faith of these,
The faith that glorifies and frees,
Thy lands call on thee, and thy seas.

If thou hast sinned, shall we forsake
Thee, or the less account us thine ?
Thy sores, thy shames on us we take.
Flies not for us thy famed ensign ?
Be ours to cleanse and to atone ;
No man this burden bears alone ;
England, our best shall be thine own.

Lift up thy cause into the light !
Put all the factious lips to shame !
Our loves, our faiths, our hopes unite
And strike into a single flame !
Whatever from without betide,
O purify the soul of pride
In us ; thy slumbers cast aside ;
And of thy sons be justified !

Laurence Binyon.

17. THE VOLUNTEER

" HE leapt to arms unbidden,
    Unneeded, over-bold ;
His face by earth is hidden,
    His heart in earth is cold.

" Curse on the reckless daring
    That could not wait the call,
The proud fantastic bearing
    That would be first to fall ! "

O tears of human passion,
  Blur not the image true ;
This was not folly's fashion,
  This was the man we knew.

Henry Newbolt.

18. MANY SISTERS TO MANY BROTHERS

WHEN we fought campaigns (in the long Christmas
    rains)
  With soldiers spread in troops on the floor,
I shot as straight as you, my losses were as few,
  My victories as many, or more.
And when in naval battle, amid cannon's rattle,
  Fleet met fleet in the bath,
My cruisers were as trim, my battleships as grim,
  My submarines cut as swift a path.
Or, when it rained too long, and the strength of the
    strong
  Surged up and broke a way with blows,
I was as fit and keen, my fists hit as clean,
  Your black eye matched my bleeding nose.
Was there a scrap or ploy in which you, the boy,
  Could better me ?   You could not climb higher,
Ride straighter, run as quick (and to smoke made
    you sick)
  . . . But I sit here, and you're under fire.

Oh, it's you that have the luck, out there in blood
    and muck :
  You were born beneath a kindly star ;

All we dreamt, I and you, you can really go and do,
  And I can't, the way things are.
In a trench you are sitting, while I am knitting
  A hopeless sock that never gets done.
Well, here's luck, my dear ;—and you've got it, no
    fear ;
  But for me . . . a war is poor fun.

                                        Rose Macaulay.

19. THE DEFENDERS

HIS wage of rest at nightfall still
    He takes, who sixty years has known
Of ploughing over Cotsall hill
    And keeping trim the Cotsall stone.

He meditates the dusk, and sees
    Folds of his wonted shepherdings
And lands of stubble and tall trees
    Becoming insubstantial things.

And does he see on Cotsall hill—
    Thrown even to the central shire—
The funnelled shapes forbidding still
    The stranger from his cottage fire?

                                        John Drinkwater.

20. THE DEAD

THESE hearts were woven of human joys and cares,
    Washed marvellously with sorrow, swift to mirth.
The years had given them kindness. Dawn was
      theirs,
    And sunset, and the colours of the earth.

These had seen movement, and heard music ; known
  Slumber and waking ; loved ; gone proudly
    friended ;
Felt the quick stir of wonder ; sat alone ;
  Touched flowers and furs, and cheeks. All this is
    ended.

There are waters blown by changing winds to laughter
And lit by the rich skies, all day.   And after,
  Frost, with a gesture, stays the waves that dance
And wandering loveliness.   He leaves a white
  Unbroken glory, a gathered radiance,
A width, a shining peace, under the night.

Rupert Brooke.

21. THE SOLDIER

IF I should die, think only this of me :
    That there's some corner of a foreign field
That is for ever England.   There shall be
  In that rich earth a richer dust concealed ;
A dust whom England bore, shaped, made aware,
  Gave, once, her flowers to love, her ways to roam,
A body of England's, breathing English air,
  Washed by the rivers, blest by suns of home.

And think, this heart, all evil shed away,
  A pulse in the eternal mind, no less
    Gives somewhere back the thoughts by England
      given ;
Her sights and sounds ; dreams happy as her day ;
  And laughter, learnt of friends ; and gentleness,
    In hearts at peace, under an English heaven.

Rupert Brooke.

22. FOR THE FALLEN

WITH proud thanksgiving, a mother for her
     children,
England mourns for her dead across the sea.
Flesh of her flesh they were, spirit of her spirit,
Fallen in the cause of the free.

Solemn the drums thrill: Death august and royal
Sings sorrow up into immortal spheres.
There is music in the midst of desolation
And a glory that shines upon our tears.

They went with songs to the battle, they were young,
Straight of limb, true of eye, steady and aglow.
They were staunch to the end against odds uncounted,
They fell with their faces to the foe.

They shall grow not old, as we that are left grow old:
Age shall not weary them, nor the years condemn.
At the going down of the sun and in the morning
We will remember them.

They mingle not with their laughing comrades again;
They sit no more at familiar tables of home;
They have no lot in our labour of the day-time:
They sleep beyond England's foam.

But where our desires are and our hopes profound,
Felt as a well-spring that is hidden from sight,
To the innermost heart of their own land they are
     known
As the stars are known to the Night;

As the stars that shall be bright when we are dust
Moving in marches upon the heavenly plain,
As the stars that are starry in the time of our dark-
    ness,
To the end, to the end, they remain.

Laurence Binyon.

23. SHADOWS AND LIGHTS

WHAT gods have met in battle to arouse
    This whirling shadow of invisible things,
These hosts that writhe amid the shattered sods ?
O Father, and O Mother of the gods,
Is there some trouble in the heavenly house ?
We who are captained by its unseen kings
Wonder what thrones are shaken in the skies,
What powers who held dominion o'er our will
Let fall the sceptre, and what destinies
The younger gods may drive us to fulfil.

Have they not swayed us, earth's invisible lords,
With whispers and with breathings from the dark ?
The very border stones of nations mark
Where silence swallowed some wild prophet's words
That rang but for an instant and were still,
Yet were so burthened with eternity,
They maddened all who heard to work their will,
To raise the lofty temple on the hill,
And many a glittering thicket of keen swords
Flashed out to make one law for land and sea,
That earth might move with heaven in company.

The cities that to myriad beauty grew
Were altars raised unto old gods who died,
And they were sacrificed in ruins to
The younger gods who took their place of pride ;
They have no brotherhood, the deified,
No high companionship of throne by throne,
But will their beauty still to be alone.

What is a nation but a multitude
United by some god-begotten mood,
Some hope of liberty or dream of power
That have not with each other brotherhood
But warred in spirit from their natal hour,
Their hatred god-begotten as their love
Reverberations of eternal strife ?
For all that fury breathed in human life,
Are ye not guilty, answer, ye above ?

Ah, no, the circle of the heavenly ones,
That ring of burning, grave, inflexible powers,
Array in harmony amid the deep
The shining legionaries of the suns,
That through their day from dawn to twilight keep
The peace of heaven, and have no feuds like ours.
The morning Stars their labours of the dawn
Close at the advent of the Solar Kings,
And these with joy their sceptres yield, withdrawn
When the still Evening Stars begin their reign,
And twilight time is thrilled with homing wings
To the All-Father being turned again.

No, not on high begin divergent ways,
The galaxies of interlinked lights
Rejoicing on each other's beauty gaze,
'Tis we who do make errant all the rays
That stream upon us from the astral heights.
Love in our thickened air too redly burns ;
And unto vanity our beauty turns ;
Wisdom, that gently whispers us to part
From evil, swells to hatred in the heart.
Dark is the shadow of invisible things
On us who look not up, whose vision fails.
The glorious shining of the heavenly kings
To mould us in their image naught avails,
They weave a robe of many-coloured fire
To garb the spirits thronging in the deep,
And in the upper air its splendours keep
Pure and unsullied, but below it trails
Darkling and glimmering in our earthly mire.

With eyes bent ever earthwards we are swayed
But by the shadows of eternal light,
And shadow against shadow is arrayed
So that one dark may dominate the night.
Though kindred are the lights that cast the shade,
We look not up, nor see how, side by side,
The high originals of all our pride
In crowned and sceptred brotherhood are throned,
Compassionate of our blindness and our hate
That own the godship but the love disowned.
Ah, let us for a little while abate
The outward roving eye, and seek within

Where spirit unto spirit is allied ;
There, in our inmost being, we may win
The joyful vision of the heavenly wise
To see the beauty in each other's eyes.

A. E.

24. BRUMANA

OH shall I never never be home again !
      Meadows of England shining in the rain
Spread wide your daisied lawns : your ramparts green
With briar fortify, with blossom screen
Till my far morning—and O streams that slow
And pure and deep through plains and playlands go,
For me your love and all your kingcups store,
And—dark militia of the southern shore,
Old fragrant friends—preserve me the last lines
Of that long saga which you sang me, pines,
When, lonely boy, beneath the chosen tree
I listened, with my eyes upon the sea.

O traitor pines, you sang what life has found
The falsest of fair tales.
Earth blew a far-horn prelude all around,
That native music of her forest home,
While from the sea's blue fields and syren dales
Shadows and light noon spectres of the foam
Riding the summer gales
On aery viols plucked an idle sound.

Hearing you sing, O trees,
Hearing you murmur, " There are older seas,
That beat on vaster sands,

Where the wise snailfish move their pearly towers
To carven rocks and sculptured promont'ries,"
Hearing you whisper, " Lands
Where blaze the unimaginable flowers."

Beneath me in the valley waves the palm,
Beneath, beyond the valley, breaks the sea ;
Beneath me sleep in mist and light and calm
Cities of Lebanon, dream-shadow-dim,
Where Kings of Tyre and Kings of Tyre did rule
In ancient days in endless dynasty,
And all around the snowy mountains swim
Like mighty swans afloat in heaven's pool.

But I will walk upon the wooded hill
Where stands a grove, O pines, of sister pines,
And when the downy twilight droops her wing
And no sea glimmers and no mountain shines
My heart shall listen still.
For pines are gossip pines the wide world through
And full of runic tales to sigh or sing.
'Tis ever sweet through pines to see the sky
Blushing a deeper gold or darker blue.
'Tis ever sweet to lie
On the dry carpet of the needles brown,
And though the fanciful green lizard stir
And windy odours light as thistledown
Breathe from the lavdanon and lavender,
Half to forget the wandering and pain,
Half to remember days that have gone by,
And dream and dream that I am home again !

James Elroy Flecker.

25. A LYKE-WAKE CAROL

GROW old and die, rich Day,
   Over some English field—
Chartered to come away
   What time to Death you yield !
Pass, frost-white ghost, and then
Come forth to banish'd men !

I see the stubble's sheen,
   The mist and ruddled leaves,
Here where the new Spring's green
   For her first rain-drops grieves.
Here beechen leaves drift red
Last week in England dead.

For English eyes' delight
   Those Autumn ghosts go free—
Ghost of the field hoar-white,
   Ghost of the crimson tree.
Grudge them not, England dear,
To us thy banished here !

Arthur Shearly Cripps.

26. A REFRAIN

TELL the tune his feet beat
   On the ground all day—
Black-burnt ground and green grass
Seamed with rocks of grey—
" England," " England," " England,"
That one word they say.

Now they tread the beech-mast,
Now the ploughland's clay,
Now the faëry ball-floor of her fields in May.
Now her red June sorrel, now her new-turned hay,
Now they keep the great road, now by sheep-path
    stray,
Still it's " England," " England,"
" England " all the way !

Arthur Shearly Cripps.

27. WHERE A ROMAN VILLA STOOD, ABOVE FREIBURG

ON alien ground, breathing an alien air,
    A Roman stood, far from his ancient home,
And gazing, murmured, " Ah, the hills are fair,
    But not the hills of Rome ! "

Descendant of a race to Romans kin,
    Where the old son of Empire stood, I stand.
The self-same rocks fold the same valley in,
    Untouched of human hand.

Over another shines the self-same star,
    Another heart with nameless longing fills,
Crying aloud, " How beautiful they are,
    But not our English hills ! "

Mary E. Coleridge.

3

28. HEIGHTS AND DEPTHS

H<small>E</small> walked in glory on the hills ;
   We dalesmen envied from afar
The heights and rose-lit pinnacles
   Which placed him nigh the evening star.

Upon the peaks they found him dead ;
   And now we wonder if he sighed
For our low grass beneath his head,
   For our rude huts, before he died.
                William Canton.

29. IN THE HIGHLANDS

I<small>N</small> the highlands, in the country places,
   Where the old plain men have rosy faces,
And the young fair maidens
   Quiet eyes;
Where essential silence cheers and blesses,
And for ever in the hill-recesses
   Her more lovely music
   Broods and dies.

O to mount again where erst I haunted;
Where the old red hills are bird-enchanted,
   And the low green meadows
   Bright with sward ;
And when even dies, the million-tinted,
And the night has come, and planets glinted,
   Lo, the valley hollow
   Lamp-bestarred !

O to dream, O to awake and wander
There, and with delight to take and render,
    Through the trance of silence,
        Quiet breath ;
Lo ! for there, among the flowers and grasses,
Only the mightier movement sounds and passes ;
    Only winds and rivers,
        Life and death.
                            Robert Louis Stevenson.

30. IN CITY STREETS

YONDER in the heather there's a bed for sleeping,
    Drink for one athirst, ripe blackberries to eat ;
Yonder in the sun the merry hares go leaping,
    And the pool is clear for travel-wearied feet.

Sorely throb my feet, a-tramping London highways,
    (Ah ! the springy moss upon a northern moor !)
Through the endless streets, the gloomy squares and
        byways,
    Homeless in the City, poor among the poor !

London streets are gold—ah, give me leaves a-glinting
    'Midst grey dykes and hedges in the autumn sun !
London water's wine, poured out for all unstinting—
    God! For the little brooks that tumble as they run !

Oh, my heart is fain to hear the soft wind blowing,
    Soughing through the fir-tops up on northern fells !
Oh, my eye's an ache to see the brown burns flowing
    Through the peaty soil and tinkling heather-bells.
                            Ada Smith.

31. MARGARET'S SONG

Too soothe and mild your lowland airs
    For one whose hope is gone :
I'm thinking of a little tarn,
    Brown, very lone.

Would now the tall swift mists could lay
    Their wet grasp on my hair,
And the great natures of the hills
    Round me friendly were.

In vain !—For taking hills your plains
    Have spoilt my soul, I think,
But would my feet were going down
    Towards the brown tarn's brink.
                    Lascelles Abercrombie.

32. TO S. R. CROCKETT

Blows the wind to-day, and the sun and the rain
    are flying,
Blows the wind on the moors to-day and now,
Where about the graves of the martyrs the whaups are
    crying,
My heart remembers how !

Grey recumbent tombs of the dead in desert places,
    Standing stones on the vacant wine-red moor,
Hills of sheep, and the homes of the silent vanished
    races,
    And winds, austere and pure :

Be it granted me to behold you again in dying,
   Hills of home ! and to hear again the call ;
Hear about the graves of the martyrs the peewees
    crying,
And hear no more at all.

              Robert Louis Stevenson.

33. CHILLINGHAM

I

THROUGH the sunny garden
   The humming bees are still ;
The fir climbs the heather,
   The heather climbs the hill.

The low clouds have riven
   A little rift through.
The hill climbs to heaven,
   Far away and blue.

II

O the high valley, the little low hill,
   And the cornfield over the sea,
The wind that rages and then lies still,
   And the clouds that rest and flee !

O the gray island in the rainbow haze,
   And the long thin spits of land,
The roughening pastures and the stony ways,
   And the golden flash of the sand !

O the red heather on the moss-wrought rock,
  And the fir-tree stiff and straight,
The shaggy old sheep-dog barking at the flock,
  And the rotten old five-barred gate!

O the brown bracken, the blackberry bough,
  The scent of the gorse in the air!
I shall love them ever as I love them now,
  I shall weary in Heaven to be there!

III

Strike, Life, a happy hour, and let me live
  But in that grace!
I shall have gathered all the world can give,
  Unending Time and Space!

Bring light and air—the thin and shining air
  Of the North land,
The light that falls on tower and garden there,
  Close to the gold sea-sand.

Bring flowers, the latest colours of the earth,
  Ere nun-like frost
Lay her hard hand upon this rainbow mirth,
  With twinkling emerald crossed.

The white star of the traveller's joy, the deep
  Empurpled rays that hide the smoky stone,
The dahlia rooted in Egyptian sleep,
  The last frail rose alone.

Let music whisper from a casement set
    By them of old,
Where the light smell of lavender may yet
    Rise from the soft loose mould.

Then shall I know, with eyes and ears awake,
    Not in bright gleams,
The joy my Heavenly Father joys to make
    For men who grieve, in dreams !
                                Mary E. Coleridge.

34. SUSSEX

G OD gave all men all earth to love,
    But since our hearts are small,
Ordained for each one spot should prove
    Beloved over all ;
That as He watched Creation's birth
    So we, in godlike mood,
May of our love create our earth
    And see that it is good.

So one shall Baltic pines content,
    As one some Surrey glade,
Or one the palm-grove's droned lament
    Before Levuka's trade.
Each to his choice, and I rejoice
    The lot has fallen to me
In a fair ground—in a fair ground—
    Yea, Sussex by the sea !

No tender-hearted garden crowns,
  No bosomed woods adorn
Our blunt, bow-headed, whale-backed Downs,
  But gnarled and writhen thorn—
Bare slopes where chasing shadows skim,
  And through the gaps revealed
Belt upon belt, the wooded, dim
  Blue goodness of the Weald.

Clean of officious fence or hedge,
  Half-wild and wholly tame,
The wise turf cloaks the white cliff edge
  As when the Romans came.
What sign of those that fought and died
  At shift of sword and sword ?
The barrow and the camp abide,
  The sunlight and the sward.

Here leaps ashore the full Sou'west
  All heavy-winged with brine,
Here lies above the folded crest
  The Channel's leaden line ;
And here the sea-fogs lap and cling,
  And here, each warning each,
The sheep-bells and the ship-bells ring
  Along the hidden beach.

We have no waters to delight
  Our broad and brookless vales—
Only the dewpond on the height
  Unfed, that never fails,

Whereby no tattered herbage tells
  Which way the season flies—
Only our close-bit thyme that smells
  Like dawn in Paradise.

Here through the strong unhampered days
  The tinkling silence thrills ;
Or little, lost, Down churches praise
  The Lord who made the hills :
But here the Old Gods guard their round,
  And, in her secret heart,
The heathen kingdom Wilfrid found
  Dreams, as she dwells, apart.

Though all the rest were all my share,
  With equal soul I'd see
Her nine-and-thirty sisters fair,
  Yet none more fair than she.
Choose ye your need from Thames to Tweed,
  And I will choose instead
Such lands as lie 'twixt Rake and Rye,
  Black Down and Beachy Head.

I will go out against the sun
  Where the rolled scarp retires,
And the Long Man of Wilmington
  Looks naked toward the shires ;
And east till doubling Rother crawls
  To find the fickle tide,
By dry and sea-forgotten walls,
  Our ports of stranded pride.

I will go north about the shaws
    And the deep ghylls that breed
Huge oaks and old, the which we hold
    No more than " Sussex weed " ;
Or south where windy Piddinghoe's
    Begilded dolphin veers,
And black beside wide-bankèd Ouse
    Lie down our Sussex steers.

So to the land our hearts we give
    Till the sure magic strike,
And Memory, Use, and Love make live
    Us and our fields alike—
That deeper than our speech and thought,
    Beyond our reason's sway,
Clay of the pit whence we were wrought
    Yearns to its fellow-clay.

God gives all men all earth to love,
    But since man's heart is small
Ordains for each one spot shall prove
    Beloved over all.
Each to his choice, and I rejoice
    The lot has fallen to me
In a fair ground—in a fair ground—
    Yea, Sussex by the sea !

Rudyard Kipling.

35. THE SOUTH COUNTRY

WHEN I am living in the Midlands,
   That are sodden and unkind,
I light my lamp in the evening :
   My work is left behind ;
And the great hills of the South Country
   Come back into my mind.

The great hills of the South Country
   They stand along the sea,
And it's there, walking in the high woods,
   That I could wish to be,
And the men that were boys when I was a boy
   Walking along with me.

The men that live in North England
   I saw them for a day :
Their hearts are set upon the waste fells,
   Their skies are fast and grey ;
From their castle-walls a man may see
   The mountains far away.

The men that live in West England
   They see the Severn strong,
A-rolling on rough water brown
   Light aspen leaves along.
They have the secret of the Rocks,
   And the oldest kind of song.

But the men that live in the South Country
   Are the kindest and most wise,
They get their laughter from the loud surf,
   And the faith in their happy eyes

Comes surely from our Sister the Spring
   When over the sea she flies ;
The violets suddenly bloom at her feet,
   She blesses us with surprise.

I never get between the pines
   But I smell the Sussex air ;
Nor I never come on a belt of sand
   But my home is there.
And along the sky the line of the Downs
   So noble and so bare.

A lost thing could I never find,
   Nor a broken thing mend :
And I fear I shall be all alone
   When I get towards the end.
Who will there be to comfort me
   Or who will be my friend ?

I will gather and carefully make my friends
   Of the men of the Sussex Weald,
They watch the stars from silent folds,
   They stiffly plough the field.
By them and the God of the South Country
   My poor soul shall be healed.

If I ever become a rich man,
   Or if ever I grow to be old,
I will build a house with deep thatch
   To shelter me from the cold,
And there shall the Sussex songs be sung
   And the story of Sussex told.

I will hold my house in the high wood,
   Within a walk of the sea,
And the men that were boys when I was a boy
   Shall sit and drink with me.
                              Hilaire Belloc.

36. CHANCLEBURY RING

SAY what you will, there is not in the world
   A nobler sight than from this upper down.
No rugged landscape here, no beauty hurled
From its Creator's hand as with a frown ;
But a green plain on which green hills look down
Trim as a garden plot.   No other hue
Can hence be seen, save here and there the brown
Of a square fallow, and the horizon's blue.
Dear checker-work of woods, the Sussex weald.
If a name thrills me yet of things of earth,
That name is thine ! How often I have fled
To thy deep hedgerows and embraced each field,
Each lag, each pasture,—fields which gave me birth
And saw my youth, and which must hold me dead.
                              Wilfrid Blunt.

37. IN ROMNEY MARSH

As I went down to Dymchurch Wall,
   I heard the South sing o'er the land ;
I saw the yellow sunlight fall
   On knolls where Norman churches stand.

And ringing shrilly, taut and lithe,
  Within the wind a core of sound,
The wire from Romney town to Hythe
  Alone its airy journey wound.

A veil of purple vapour flowed
  And trailed its fringe along the Straits ;
The upper air like sapphire glowed ;
  And roses filled Heaven's central gates.

Masts in the offing wagged their tops ;
  The swinging waves pealed on the shore ;
The saffron beach, all diamond drops
  And beads of surge, prolonged the roar.

As I came up from Dymchurch Wall,
  I saw above the Down's low crest
The crimson brands of sunset fall,
  Flicker and fade from out the west.

Night sank : like flakes of silver fire
  The stars in one great shower came down ;
Shrill blew the wind ; and shrill the wire
  Rang out from Hythe to Romney town.

The darkly shining salt sea drops
  Streamed as the waves clashed on the shore ;
The beach, with all its organ stops
  Pealing again, prolonged the roar.
                  John Davidson.

38. A CINQUE PORT

BELOW the down the stranded town
  What may betide forlornly waits,
With memories of smoky skies,
  When Gallic navies crossed the straits ;
When waves with fire and blood grew bright,
And cannon thundered through the night.

With swinging stride the rhythmic tide
  Bore to the harbour barque and sloop ;
Across the bar the ship of war,
  In castled stern and lanterned poop,
Came up with conquests on her lee,
The stately mistress of the sea.

Where argosies have wooed the breeze,
  The simple sheep are feeding now ;
And near and far across the bar
  The ploughman whistles at the plough ;
Where once the long waves washed the shore,
Larks from their lowly lodgings soar.

Below the down the stranded town
  Hears far away the rollers beat ;
About the wall the seabirds call ;
  The salt wind murmurs through the street ;
Forlorn the sea's forsaken bride
Awaits the end that shall betide.

John Davidson.

39. ESSEX

I GO through the fields of blue water
    On the South road of the sea.
High to North the East-Country
    Holds her green fields to me—
For she that I gave over,
    Gives not over me.

Last night I lay at Good Easter
    Under a hedge I knew,
Last night beyond High Easter
    I trod the May-floors blue—
Till from the sea the sun came
    Bidding me wake and rue.

Roding (that names eight churches)—
    Banks with the paigles dight—
Chelmer whose mill and willows
    Keep one red tower in sight—
Under the Southern Cross run
    Beside the ship to-night.

Ah! I may not seek back now,
    Neither be turned nor stayed.
Yet should I live, I'd seek her,
    Once that my vows are paid!
And should I die I'd haunt her—
    I being what God made!

England has greater counties—
    Their peace to hers is small.

Low hills, rich fields, calm rivers,
    In Essex seek them all,—
Essex, where I that found them
    Found to lose them all !
                                Arthur Shearly Cripps.

40. A TOWN WINDOW

BEYOND my window in the night
        Is but a drab inglorious street,
Yet there the frost and clean starlight
    As over Warwick woods are sweet.

Under the grey drift of the town
    The crocus works among the mould
As eagerly as those that crown
    The Warwick spring in flame and gold.

And when the tramway down the hill
    Across the cobbles moans and rings,
There is about my window-sill
    The tumult of a thousand wings.
                                John Drinkwater.

41. MAMBLE

I NEVER went to Mamble
        That lies above the Teme,
So I wonder who's in Mamble,
    And whether people seem
Who breed and brew along there
    As lazy as the name,
And whether any song there
    Sets alehouse wits aflame.

4

The finger-post says Mamble,
　　And that is all I know
Of the narrow road to Mamble,
　　And should I turn and go
To that place of lazy token,
　　That lies above the Teme,
There might be a Mamble broken
　　That was lissom in a dream.

So leave the road to Mamble
　　And take another road
To as good a place as Mamble
　　Be it lazy as a toad ;
Who travels Worcester county
　　Takes any place that comes
When April tosses bounty
　　To the cherries and the plums.

　　　　　　　　　　John Drinkwater.

42. PLYMOUTH HARBOUR

OH, what know they of harbours
　　Who toss not on the sea !
They tell of fairer havens,
　　But none so fair there be

As Plymouth town outstretching
　　Her quiet arms to me ;
Her breast's broad welcome spreading
　　From Mewstone to Penlee.

Ah, with this home-thought, darling,
  Come crowding thoughts of thee.
Oh, what know they of harbours
  Who toss not on the sea !

Ernest Radford.

43. OXFORD

I CAME to Oxford in the light
    Of a spring-coloured afternoon ;
Some clouds were grey and some were white,
And all were blown to such a tune
Of quiet rapture in the sky,
I laughed to see them laughing by.

I had been dreaming in the train
    With thoughts at random from my book ;
I looked, and read, and looked again,
    And suddenly to greet my look
Oxford shone up with every tower
Aspiring sweetly like a flower.

Home turn the feet of men that seek,
    And home the hearts of children turn,
And none can teach the hour to speak
    What every hour is free to learn ;
And all discover, late or soon,
Their golden Oxford afternoon.

Gerald Gould.

44. ALMA MATER

KNOW you her secret none can utter ?
   Hers of the Book, the tripled Crown ?
Still on the spire the pigeons flutter,
   Still by the gateway flits the gown ;
Still on the street, from corbel and gutter,
   Faces of stone look down.

Faces of stone, and stonier faces—
   Some from library windows wan
Forth on her gardens, her green spaces,
   Peer and turn to their books anon.
Hence, my Muse, from the green oases
   Gather the tent, begone !

Nay, should she by the pavement linger
   Under the rooms where once she played,
Who from the feast would rise to fling her
   One poor *sou* for her serenade ?
One short laugh for the antic finger
   Thrumming a lute-string frayed ?

Once, my dear—but the world was young then—
   Magdalen elms and Trinity limes—
Lissom the blades and the backs that swung then,
   Eight good men in the good old times—
Careless we, and the chorus flung then
   Under St. Mary's chimes !

Reins lay loose and the ways led random—
   Christ Church meadow and Iffley track,

" Idleness horrid and dog-cart " (tandem),
   Aylesbury grind and Bicester pack—
Pleasant our lines, and faith ! we scanned 'em ;
   Having that artless knack.

Come, old limmer, the times grow colder ;
   Leaves of the creeper redden and fall.
Was it a hand then clapped my shoulder ?—
   Only the wind by the chapel wall !
Dead leaves drift on the lute . . . So fold her
   Under the faded shawl.

Never we wince, though none deplore us,
   We who go reaping that we sowed ;
Cities at cockcrow wake before us—
   Hey, for the lilt of the London road !
One look back, and a rousing chorus !
   Never a palinode !

Still on her spire the pigeons hover ;
   Still by her gateway haunts the gown.
Ah, but her secret ?   You, young lover,
   Drumming her old ones forth from town,
Know you the secret none discover ?
   Tell it—when *you* go down.

Yet if at length you seek her, prove her,
   Lean to her whispers never so nigh ;
Yet if at last not less her lover
   You in your hansom leave the High ;
Down from her towers a ray shall hover—
   Touch you, a passer-by.

Arthur Quiller-Couch.

45. FROM "DEDICATORY ODE"

I WILL not try the reach again,
   I will not set my sail alone,
To moor a boat bereft of men
   At Yarnton's tiny docks of stone.

But I will sit beside the fire,
   And put my hand before my eyes,
And trace, to fill my heart's desire,
   The last of all our Odysseys.

The quiet evening kept her tryst :
   Beneath an open sky we rode,
And passed into a wandering mist
   Along the perfect Evenlode.

The tender Evenlode that makes
   Her meadows hush to hear the sound
Of waters mingling in the brakes,
   And binds my heart to English ground.

A lovely river, all alone,
   She lingers in the hills and holds
A hundred little towns of stone,
   Forgotten in the western wolds.

                Hilaire Belloc.

46. THE DEVOURERS

CAMBRIDGE town is a beleaguered city ;
   For south and north, like a sea,
There beat on its gates, without haste or pity,
   The downs and the fen country.

Cambridge towers, so old, so wise,
  They were builded but yesterday,
Watched by sleepy gray secret eyes
  That smiled as at children's play.

Roads south of Cambridge run into the waste,
  Where learning and lamps are not,
And the pale downs tumble, blind, chalk-faced,
  And the brooding churches squat.

Roads north of Cambridge march through a plain
  Level like the traitor sea.
It will swallow its ships, and turn and smile again—
  The insatiable fen country.

Lest the downs and the fens should eat Cambridge up,
  And its towers be tossed and thrown,
And its rich wine drunk from its broken cup,
  And its beauty no more known—

Let us come, you and I, where the roads run blind,
  Out beyond the transient city,
That our love, mingling with earth, may find
  Her imperishable heart of pity.

                              Rose Macaulay.

47. THE OLD VICARAGE, GRANTCHESTER

Café des Westens, Berlin

JUST now the lilac is in bloom,
    All before my little room ;
And in my flower-beds, I think,

Smile the carnation and the pink ;
And down the borders, well I know,
The poppy and the pansy blow . . .
Oh ! there the chestnuts, summer through,
Beside the river make for you
A tunnel of green gloom, and sleep
Deeply above ; and green and deep
The stream mysterious glides beneath,
Green as a dream and deep as death.—
Oh, damn ! I know it ! and I know
How the May fields all golden show,
And when the day is young and sweet,
Gild gloriously the bare feet
That run to bathe . . .
                              Du lieber Gott !

Here am I, sweating, sick, and hot,
And there the shadowed waters fresh
Lean up to embrace the naked flesh.
Temperamentvoll German Jews
Drink beer around ; and *there* the dews
Are soft beneath a morn of gold.
Here tulips bloom as they are told ;
Unkempt about those hedges blows
An English unofficial rose ;
And there the unregulated sun
Slopes down to rest when day is done,
And wakes a vague unpunctual star,
A slippered Hesper ; and there are
Meads towards Haslingfield and Coton
Where *das Betreten*'s not *verboten.* . . .

εἴθε γενοίμην . . . would I were
In Grantchester, in Grantchester !—
Some, it may be, can get in touch
With Nature there, or Earth, or such.
And clever modern men have seen
A Faun a-peeping through the green,
And felt the Classics were not dead,
To glimpse a Naiad's reedy head,
Or hear the Goat-foot piping low . . .
But these are things I do not know.
I only know that you may lie
Day long and watch the Cambridge sky,
And, flower-lulled in sleepy grass,
Hear the cool lapse of hours pass,
Until the centuries blend and blur
In Grantchester, in Grantchester . . .
Still in the dawnlit waters cool
His ghostly Lordship swims his pool,
And tries the strokes, essays the tricks,
Long learnt on Hellespont, or Styx ;
Dan Chaucer hears his river still
Chatter beneath a phantom mill ;
Tennyson notes, with studious eye,
How Cambridge waters hurry by . . .
And in that garden, black and white
Creep whispers through the grass all night ;
And spectral dance, before the dawn,
A hundred Vicars down the lawn ;
Curates, long dust, will come and go
On lissom, clerical, printless toe ;
And oft between the boughs is seen

The sly shade of a Rural Dean . . .
Till, at a shiver in the skies,
Vanishing with Satanic cries,
The prim ecclesiastic rout
Leaves but a startled sleeper-out,
Grey heavens, the first bird's drowsy calls,
The falling house that never falls.

God ! I will pack, and take a train,
And get me to England once again !
For England's the one land, I know,
Where men with Splendid Hearts may go ;
And Cambridgeshire, of all England,
The shire for Men who Understand ;
And of *that* district I prefer
The lovely hamlet Grantchester.
For Cambridge people rarely smile,
Being urban, squat, and packed with guile ;
And Royston men in the far South
Are black and fierce and strange of mouth ;
At Over they fling oaths at one,
And worse than oaths at Trumpington,
And Ditton girls are mean and dirty,
And there's none in Harston under thirty,
And folks in Shelford and those parts,
Have twisted lips and twisted hearts,
And Barton men make cockney rhymes,
And Coton's full of nameless crimes,
And things are done you'd not believe
At Madingley on Christmas Eve.
Strong men have run for miles and miles

When one from Cherry Hinton smiles ;
Strong men have blanched and shot their wives
Rather than send them to St. Ives ;
Strong men have cried like babes, bydam,
To hear what happened at Babraham.
But Grantchester ! ah, Grantchester !
There's peace and holy quiet there,
Great clouds along pacific skies,
And men and women with straight eyes,
Lithe children lovelier than a dream,
A bosky wood, a slumbrous stream,
And little kindly winds that creep
Round twilight corners, half asleep.
In Grantchester their skins are white,
They bathe by day, they bathe by night ;
The women there do all they ought ;
The men observe the Rules of Thought.
They love the Good ; they worship Truth ;
They laugh uproariously in youth ;
(And when they get to feeling old,
They up and shoot themselves, I'm told). . .

Ah God ! to see the branches stir
Across the moon at Grantchester !
To smell the thrilling-sweet and rotten,
Unforgettable, unforgotten
River smell, and hear the breeze
Sobbing in the little trees.
Say, do the elm-clumps greatly stand,
Still guardians of that holy land ?
The chestnuts shade, in reverend dream,

The yet unacademic stream ?
Is dawn a secret shy and cold
Anadyomene, silver-gold ?
And sunset still a golden sea
From Haslingfield to Madingley ?
And after, ere the night is born,
Do hares come out about the corn ?
Oh, is the water sweet and cool
Gentle and brown, above the pool ?
And laughs the immortal river still
Under the mill, under the mill ?
Say, is there Beauty yet to find ?
And Certainty ? and Quiet kind ?
Deep meadows yet, for to forget
The lies, and truths, and pain ? . . . oh ! yet
Stands the Church clock at ten to three ?
And is there honey still for tea ?

Rupert Brooke.

48. DAYS THAT HAVE BEEN

CAN I forget the sweet days that have been,
    When poetry first began to warm my blood ;
When from the hills of Gwent I saw the earth
    Burned into two by Severn's silver flood :

When I would go alone at night to see
    The moonlight, like a big white butterfly,
Dreaming on that old castle near Caerleon,
    While at its side the Usk went softly by :

When I would stare at lovely clouds in Heaven,
  Or watch them when reported by deep streams ;
When feeling pressed like thunder, but would not
  Break into that grand music of my dreams ?

Can I forget the sweet days that have been,
  The villages so green I have been in ;
Llantarnam, Magor, Malpas, and Llanwern,
  Liswery, old Caerleon, and Alteryn ?

Can I forget the banks of Malpas Brook,
  Or Ebbw's voice in such a wild delight,
As on he dashed with pebbles in his throat,
  Gurgling towards the sea with all his might ?

Ah, when I see a leafy village now
  I sigh and ask it for Llantarnam's green ;
I ask each river where is Ebbw's voice—
  In memory of the sweet days that have been.
                              William H. Davies.

49. THE LAKE ISLE OF INNISFREE

I WILL arise and go now, and go to Innisfree,
  And a small cabin build there, of clay and
    wattles made ;
Nine bean rows will I have there, a hive for the honey
    bee,
And live alone in the bee-loud glade.

And I shall have some peace there, for peace comes
　　dropping slow,
Dropping from the veils of the morning to where the
　　cricket sings ;
There midnight's all a glimmer, and noon a purple
　　glow,
And evening full of the linnet's wings.

I will arise and go now, for always night and day
I hear lake water lapping with low sounds by the
　　shore ;
While I stand on the roadway, or on the pavements
　　gray,
I hear it in the deep heart's core.

W. B. Yeats.

50. THE FLOWERS

*B*UY *my English posies !*
　　Kent and Surrey may—
Violets of the Undercliff
　　Wet with Channel spray ;
Cowslips from a Devon combe—
　　Midland furze afire—
Buy my English posies,
　　And I'll sell your heart's desire !

Buy my English posies !
　　You that scorn the may,
Won't you greet a friend from home
　　Half the world away ?

Green against the draggled drift,
    Faint and frail and first—
Buy my Northern blood-root
    And I'll know where you were nursed :

Robin down the logging-road whistles, " Come to
    me ! "
Spring has found the maple-grove, the sap is running
    free ;
All the winds of Canada call the ploughing-rain.
Take the flower and turn the hour, and kiss your love
    again !

    Buy my English posies !
        Here's to match your need—
    Buy a tuft of royal heath,
        Buy a bunch of weed
    White as sand of Muysenberg
        Spun before the gale—
    Buy my heath and lilies
        And I'll tell you whence you hail !

Under hot Constantia broad the vineyards lie—
Throned and thorned the aching berg props the speck-
    less sky—
Slow below the Wynberg firs trails the tilted wain—
Take the flower and turn the hour, and kiss your love
    again.

    Buy my English posies !
        You that will not turn—
    Buy my hot-wood clematis,
        Buy a frond o' fern

Gather'd where the Erskine leaps
  Down the road to Lorne—
Buy my Christmas creeper
  And I'll say where you were born !

West away from Melbourne dust holidays begin—
They that mock at Paradise woo at Cora Lynn—
Through the great South Otway gums sings the great
    South Main—
Take the flower and turn the hour, and kiss your love
    again.

Buy my English posies !
  Here's your choice unsold !
Buy a blood-red myrtle-bloom,
  Buy the kowhai's gold
Flung for gift on Taupo's face,
  Sign that spring is come—
Buy my clinging myrtle
  And I'll give you back your home !

Broom behind the windy town ; pollen o' the pine—
Bell-bird in the leafy deep where the *ratas* twine—
Fern above the saddle-bow, flax upon the plain—
Take the flower and turn the hour, and kiss your love
    again.

Buy my English posies !
  Ye that have your own
Buy them for a brother's sake
  Overseas, alone.

Weed ye trample underfoot
Floods his heart abrim—
Bird ye never heeded,
O, she calls his dead to him.

Far and far our homes are set round the Seven Seas ;
Woe for us if we forget, we that hold by these !
Unto each his mother-beach, bloom and bird and
land—
Masters of the Seven Seas, oh, love and understand.
Rudyard Kipling.

51. THE HOUSE BEAUTIFUL

A NAKED house, a naked moor,
  A shivering pool before the door,
A garden bare of flowers and fruit
And poplars at the garden foot :
Such is the place that I live in,
Bleak without and bare within.

Yet shall your ragged moor receive
The incomparable pomp of eve,
And the cold glories of the dawn
Behind your shivering trees be drawn ;
And when the wind from place to place
Doth the unmoored cloud-galleons chase,
Your garden gloom and gleam again,
With leaping sun, with glancing rain.
Here shall the wizard moon ascend
The heavens, in the crimson end

5

Of day's declining splendour ; here
The army of the stars appear.
The neighbour hollows dry or wet,
Spring shall with tender flowers beset ;
And oft the morning muser see
Larks rising from the broomy lea,
And every fairy wheel and thread
Of cobweb dew-bediamonded.
When daisies go, shall winter time
Silver the simple grass with rime ;
Autumnal frosts enchant the pool
And make the cart-ruts beautiful ;
And when snow-bright the moor expands,
How shall your children clap their hands !
To make this earth our hermitage,
A cheerful and a changeful page,
God's bright and intricate device
Of days and seasons doth suffice.

Robert Louis Stevenson.

52. THE OLD LOVE

OUT of my door I step into
    The country, all her scent and dew,
Nor travel there by a hard road,
Dusty and far from my abode.

The country washes to my door
Green miles on miles in soft uproar,
The thunder of the woods, and then
The backwash of green surf again.

Beyond the feverfew and stocks,
The guelder-rose and hollyhocks;
Outside my trellised porch a tree
Of lilac frames a sky for me.

A stretch of primrose and pale green
To hold the tender Hesper in;
Hesper that by the moon makes pale
Her silver keel and silver sail.

The country silence wraps me quite,
Silence and song and pure delight;
The country beckons all the day
Smiling, and but a step away.

This is that country seen across
How many a league of love and loss,
Prayed for and longed for, and as far
As fountains in the desert are.

This is that country at my door,
Whose fragrant airs run on before,
And call me when the first birds stir
In the green wood to walk with her.

Katharine Tynan.

53. EARLY MORN

WHEN I did wake this morn from sleep,
  It seemed I heard birds in a dream;
Then I arose to take the air—
  The lovely air that made birds scream;
Just as a green hill launched the ship
Of gold, to take its first clear dip.

And it began its journey then,
  As I came forth to take the air ;
The timid Stars had vanished quite,
  The Moon was dying with a stare ;
Horses, and kine, and sheep were seen,
As still as pictures, in fields green.

It seemed as though I had surprised
  And trespassed in a golden world
That should have passed while men still slept !
  The joyful birds, the ship of gold,
The horses, kine, and sheep did seem
As they would vanish for a dream.

William H. Davies.

54. THE HILL PINES WERE SIGHING

THE hill pines were sighing,
  O'ercast and chill was the day :
A mist in the valley lying
Blotted the pleasant May.

But deep in the glen's bosom
Summer slept in the fire
Of the odorous gorse-blossom
And the hot scent of the brier.

A ribald cuckoo clamoured,
And out of the copse the stroke
Of the iron axe that hammered
The iron heart of the oak.

Anon a sound appalling,
As a hundred years of pride
Crashed, in the silence falling :
And the shadowy pine-trees sighed.

Robert Bridges.

55. THE CHOICE

WHEN skies are blue and days are bright
A kitchen-garden's my delight,
Set round with rows of decent box
And blowsy girls of hollyhocks.

Before the lark his Lauds hath done
And ere the corncrake's southward gone ;
Before the thrush good-night hath said
And the young Summer's put to bed.

The currant-bushes' spicy smell,
Homely and honest, likes me well,
The while on strawberries I feast,
And raspberries the sun hath kissed.

Beans all a-blowing by a row
Of hives that great with honey go,
With mignonette and heaths to yield
The plundering bee his honey-field.

Sweet herbs in plenty, blue borage
And the delicious mint and sage,
Rosemary, marjoram, and rue,
And thyme to scent the winter through.

Here are small apples growing round,
And apricots all golden-gowned,
And plums that presently will flush
And show their bush a Burning Bush.

Cherries in nets against the wall,
Where Master Thrush his madrigal
Sings, and makes oath a churl is he
Who grudges cherries for a fee.

Lavender, sweet-briar, orris.   Here
Shall Beauty make her pomander,
Her sweet-balls for to lay in clothes
That wrap her as the leaves the rose.

Take roses red and lilies white,
A kitchen garden's my delight;
Its gillyflowers and phlox and cloves,
And its tall cote of irised doves.

Katharine Tynan.

56. THERE IS A HILL

THERE is a hill beside the silver Thames,
    Shady with birch and beech and odorous pine :
And brilliant underfoot with thousand gems
Steeply the thickets to his floods decline.
        Straight trees in every place
        Their thick tops interlace,
And pendent branches trail their foliage fine
        Upon his watery face.

Swift from the sweltering pasturage he flows :
His stream, alert to seek the pleasant shade,
Pictures his gentle purpose, as he goes
Straight to the caverned pool his toil has made.
    His winter floods lay bare
    The stout roots in the air :
His summer streams are cool, when they have played
    Among their fibrous hair.

A rushy island guards the sacred bower,
And hides it from the meadow, where in peace
The lazy cows wrench many a scented flower,
Robbing the golden market of the bees :
    And laden barges float
    By banks of myosote ;
And scented flag and golden flower-de-lys
    Delay the loitering boat.

And on this side the island, where the pool
Eddies away, are tangled mass on mass
The water-weeds, that net the fishes cool,
And scarce allow a narrow stream to pass ;
    Where spreading crowfoot mars
    The drowning nenuphars,
Waving the tassels of her silken grass
    Below her silver stars.

But in the purple pool there nothing grows,
Not the white water-lily spoked with gold ;

Though best she loves the hollows, and well knows
On quiet streams her broad shields to unfold :
    Yet should her roots but try
    Within these deeps to lie,
Not her long-reaching stalk could ever hold
    Her waxen head so high.

Sometimes an angler comes, and drops his hook
Within its hidden depths, and 'gainst a tree
Leaning his rod, reads in some pleasant book,
Forgetting soon his pride of fishery ;
    And dreams, or falls asleep,
    While curious fishes peep
About his nibbled bait, or scornfully
    Dart off and rise and leap.

And sometimes a slow figure 'neath the trees,
In ancient-fashioned smock, with tottering care
Upon a staff propping his weary knees,
May by the pathway of the forest fare :
    As from a buried day
    Across the mind will stray
Some perishing mute shadow,—and unaware
    He passeth on his way.

Else, he that wishes solitude is safe,
Whether he bathe at morning in the stream :
Or lead his love there when the hot hours chafe
The meadows, busy with a blurring steam ;
    Or watch, as fades the light,
    The gibbous moon grow bright,
Until her magic rays dance in a dream,
    And glorify the night.

Where is this bower beside the silver Thames ?
O pool and flowery thickets, hear my vow !
O trees of freshest foliage and straight stems,
No sharer of my secret I allow :
    Lest ere I come the while
    Strange feet your shades defile ;
Or lest the burly oarsman turn his prow
    Within your guardian isle.

Robert Bridges.

57. BAB-LOCK-HYTHE

In the time of wild roses
   As up Thames we travelled
Where 'mid water-weeds ravelled
The lily uncloses,

To his old shores the river
A new song was singing,
And young shoots were springing
On old roots for ever.

Dog-daisies were dancing,
And flags flamed in cluster,
On the dark stream a lustre
Now blurred and now glancing.

A tall reed down-weighing
The sedge-warbler fluttered ;
One sweet note he uttered,
Then left it soft-swaying.

By the bank's sandy hollow
My dipt oars went beating,
And past our bows fleeting
Blue-backed shone the swallow.

High woods, heron-haunted,
Rose, changed, as we rounded
Old hills greenly mounded,
To meadows enchanted.

A dream ever moulded
Afresh for our wonder,
Still opening asunder
For the stream many-folded ;

Till sunset was rimming
The West with pale flushes;
Behind the black rushes
The last light was dimming ;

And the lonely stream, hiding
Shy birds, grew more lonely,
And with us was only
The noise of our gliding.

In cloud of gray weather
The evening o'erdarkened,
In the stillness we hearkened ;
Our hearts sang together.

Laurence Binyon.

58. ROWER'S CHANT

Row till the land dip 'neath
   The sea from view.
Row till a land peep up,
A home for you.

Row till the mast sing songs
Welcome and sweet.
Row till the waves, out-stripped,
Give up dead beat.

Row till the sea-nymphs rise
To ask you why
Rowing you tarry not
To hear them sigh.

Row till the stars grow bright
Like certain eyes.
Row till the noon be high
As hopes you prize.

Row till you harbour in
All longing's port.
Row till you find all things
For which you sought.

              T. Sturge Moore.

59. FAREWELL

Not soon shall I forget—a sheet
   Of golden water, cold and sweet,
The young moon with her head in veils
Of silver, and the nightingales.

A wain of hay came up the lane—
O fields I shall not walk again,
And trees I shall not see, so still
Against a sky of daffodil!

Fields where my happy heart had rest,
And where my heart was heaviest,
I shall remember them at peace
Drenched in moon-silver like a fleece.

The golden water sweet and cold,
The moon of silver and of gold,
The dew upon the gray grass-spears,
I shall remember them with tears.

                              Katharine Tynan.

60. A SHIP, AN ISLE, A SICKLE MOON

A SHIP, an isle, a sickle moon—
       With few but with how splendid stars
The mirrors of the sea are strewn
Between their silver bars!

      *   *   *   *   *

An isle beside an isle she lay,
The pale ship anchored in the bay,
While in the young moon's port of gold
A star-ship—as the mirrors told—
Put forth its great and lonely light
To the unreflecting Ocean, Night,

And still, a ship upon her seas,
The isle and the island cypresses
Went sailing on without the gale :
And still there moved the moon so pale,
A crescent ship without a sail !

James Elroy Flecker.

61. NOD

SOFTLY along the road of evening,
   In a twilight dim with rose,
Wrinkled with age, and drenched with dew
   Old Nod, the shepherd, goes.

His drowsy flock streams on before him,
   Their fleeces charged with gold,
To where the sun's last beam leans low
   On Nod the shepherd's fold.

The hedge is quick and green with briar,
   From their sand the conies creep ;
And all the birds that fly in heaven
   Flock singing home to sleep.

His lambs outnumber a noon's roses,
   Yet, when night's shadows fall,
His blind old sheep-dog, Slumber-soon,
   Misses not one of all.

His are the quiet steeps of dreamland,
   The waters of no-more-pain,
His ram's bell rings 'neath an arch of stars,
   " Rest, rest, and rest again."

Walter de la Mare.

62. CHIMES

Brief, on a flying night,
   From the shaken tower,
A flock of bells take flight,
   And go with the hour.

Like birds from the cote to the gales,
   Abrupt—O hark !
A fleet of bells set sails,
   And go to the dark.

Sudden the cold airs swing.
   Alone, aloud,
A verse of bells takes wing
   And flies with the cloud.

Alice Meynell.

63. SPRING GOETH ALL IN WHITE

Spring goeth all in white,
   Crowned with milk-white may :
In fleecy flocks of light
O'er heaven the white clouds stray :

White butterflies in the air ;
White daisies prank the ground :
The cherry and hoary pear
Scatter their snow around.

Robert Bridges.

64. ST. VALENTINE'S DAY

To-day, all day, I rode upon the down,
  With hounds and horsemen, a brave company.
On this side in its glory lay the sea,
On that the Sussex weald, a sea of brown.
The wind was light, and brightly the sun shone,
And still we galloped on from gorse to gorse.
And once, when checked, a thrush sang, and my
    horse
Pricked his quick ears as to a sound unknown.
I knew the Spring was come. I knew it even
Better than all by this, that through my chase
In bush and stone and hill and sea and heaven
I seemed to see and follow still your face.
Your face my quarry was. For it I rode,
My horse a thing of wings, myself a god.

Wilfrid Blunt.

65. A DAY IN SUSSEX

The dove did lend me wings. I fled away
  From the loud world which long had troubled
    me.
Oh lightly did I flee when hoyden May
Threw her wild mantle on the hawthorn-tree.
I left the dusty high-road, and my way
Was through deep meadows, shut with copses fair.
A choir of thrushes poured its roundelay
From every hedge and every thicket there.
Mild, moon-faced kine looked on, where in the grass
All heaped with flowers I lay, from noon till eve.

And hares unwitting close to me did pass,
And still the birds sang, and I could not grieve.
Oh what a blessed thing that evening was !
Peace, music, twilight, all that could deceive
A soul to joy or lull a heart to peace.
It glimmers yet across whole years like these.

Wilfrid Blunt.

66. ODE IN MAY

L ET me go forth, and share
          The overflowing Sun
    With one wise friend, or one
Better than wise, being fair,
Where the pewit wheels and dips
    On heights of bracken and ling,
And Earth, unto her leaflet tips,
    Tingles with the Spring.

What is so sweet and dear
    As a prosperous morn in May,
    The confident prime of the day,
And the dauntless youth of the year,
When nothing that asks for bliss,
    Asking aright, is denied,
And half of the world a bridegroom is,
    And half of the world a bride ?

The Song of Mingling flows,
    Grave, ceremonial, pure,
    As once, from lips that endure,
The cosmic descant rose,

When the temporal lord of life,
   Going his golden way,
Had taken a wondrous maid to wife
   That long had said him nay.

For of old the Sun, our sire,
   Came wooing the mother of men,
   Earth, that was virginal then,
Vestal fire to his fire.
Silent her bosom and coy,
   But the strong god sued and pressed ;
And born of their starry nuptial joy
   Are all that drink of her breast.

And the triumph of him that begot,
   And the travail of her that bore,
   Behold they are evermore
As warp and weft in our lot.
We are children of splendour and flame,
   Of shuddering, also, and tears.
Magnificent out of the dust we came,
   And abject from the Spheres.

O bright irresistible lord !
   We are fruit of Earth's womb, each one,
   And fruit of thy loins, O Sun,
Whence first was the seed outpoured.
To thee as our Father we bow,
   Forbidden thy Father to see,
Who is older and greater than thou, as thou
   Art greater and older than we.

6

Thou art but as a word of his speech,
   Thou art but as a wave of his hand ;
   Thou art brief as a glitter of sand
'Twixt tide and tide on his beach ;
Thou art less than a spark of his fire,
   Or a moment's mood of his soul :
Thou art lost in the notes on the lips of his choir
   That chant the chant of the Whole.
                     William Watson.

67. THE SCARECROW

ALL winter through I bow my head
   Beneath the driving rain ;
The North wind powders me with snow
   And blows me black again ;
At midnight 'neath a maze of stars
   I flame with glittering rime,
And stand, above the stubble, stiff
   As mail at morning-prime.
But when that child, called Spring, and all
   His host of children, come,
Scattering their buds and dew upon
   These acres of my home,
Some rapture in my rags awakes ;
   I lift void eyes and scan
The skies for crows, those ravening foes,
   Of my strange master, Man.
I watch him striding lank behind
   His clashing team, and know
Soon will the wheat swish body high
   Where once lay sterile snow ;

Soon shall I gaze across a sea
  Of sun-begotten grain,
Which my unflinching watch hath sealed
  For harvest once again.

Walter de la Mare.

68. THE VAGABOND

GIVE to me the life I love,
  Let the lave go by me,
Give the jolly heaven above
  And the byway nigh me.
Bed in the bush with stars to see,
  Bread I dip in the river—
There's the life for a man like me,
  There's the life for ever.

Let the blow fall soon or late,
  Let what will be o'er me ;
Give the face of earth around
  And the road before me.
Wealth I seek not, hope nor love,
  Nor a friend to know me ;
All I seek, the heaven above
  And the road below me.

Or let autumn fall on me
  Where afield I linger,
Silencing the bird on tree,
  Biting the blue finger.
White as meal the frosty field—
  Warm the fireside haven—
Not to autumn will I yield,
  Not to winter even !

Let the blow fall soon or late,
Let what will be o'er me ;
Give the face of earth around
And the road before me.
Wealth I ask not, hope nor love,
Nor a friend to know me ;
All I ask, the heaven above
And the road below me.

Robert Louis Stevenson.

69. TEWKESBURY ROAD

IT is good to be out on the road, and going one
knows not where,
Going through meadow and village, one knows not
whither nor why ;
Through the grey light drift of the dust, in the keen
cool rush of the air,
Under the flying white clouds, and the broad blue
lift of the sky.

And to halt at the chattering brook, in the tall green
fern at the brink
Where the harebell grows, and the gorse, and the
foxgloves purple and white ;
Where the shy-eyed delicate deer come down in a
troop to drink
When the stars are mellow and large at the coming
on of the night.

O, to feel the beat of the rain, and the homely smell
  of the earth,
  Is a tune for the blood to jig to, a joy past power
  of words ;
And the blessed green comely meadows are all a-ripple
  with mirth
  At the noise of the lambs at play and the dear wild
  cry of the birds.

John Masefield.

70. TO A LADY SEEN FROM THE TRAIN

O WHY do you walk through the fields in gloves,
  Missing so much and so much ?
O fat white woman whom nobody loves,
Why do you walk through the fields in gloves,
When the grass is soft as the breast of doves
  And shivering-sweet to the touch ?
O why do you walk through the fields in gloves,
  Missing so much and so much ?

Frances Cornford.

71. I WILL MAKE YOU BROOCHES

I WILL make you brooches and toys for your delight
  Of bird-song at morning and star-shine at night.
I will make a palace fit for you and me
Of green days in forests and blue days at sea.

I will make my kitchen, and you shall keep your
  room,
Where white flows the river and bright blows the
  broom,

And you shall wash your linen and keep your body
    white
In rainfall at morning and dewfall at night.

And this shall be for music when no one else is near,
The fine song for singing, the rare song to hear !
That only I remember, that only you admire,
Of the broad road that stretches and the roadside
    fire.

                    Robert Louis Stevenson.

72. JUGGLING JERRY

PITCH here the tent, while the old horse grazes :
    By the old hedge-side we'll halt a stage.
It's nigh my last above the daisies :
    My next leaf 'll be man's blank page.
Yes, my old girl ! and it's no use crying :
    Juggler, constable, king, must bow.
One that outjuggles all 's been spying
    Long to have me, and he has me now.

We've travelled times to this old common :
    Often we've hung our pots in the gorse.
We've had a stirring life, old woman !
    You, and I, and the old grey horse.
Races, and fairs, and royal occasions,
    Found us coming to their call :
Now they'll miss us at our stations :
    There's a Juggler outjuggles all !

Up goes the lark, as if all were jolly !
  Over the duck-pond the willow shakes.
Easy to think that grieving's folly,
  When the hand's firm as driven stakes !
Ay, when we're strong, and braced, and manful,
  Life's a sweet fiddle : but we're a batch
Born to become the Great Juggler's han'ful :
  Balls he shies up, and is safe to catch.

Here's where the lads of the village cricket :
  I was a lad not wide from here :
Couldn't I whip off the bail from the wicket ?
  Like an old world those days appear !
Donkey, sheep, geese, and thatched ale-house—I know
    them !
  They are old friends of my halts, and seem,
Somehow, as if kind thanks I owe them :
  Juggling don't hinder the heart's esteem.

Juggling's no sin, for we must have victual :
  Nature allows us to bait for the fool.
Holding one's own makes us juggle no little ;
  But, to increase it, hard juggling's the rule.
You that are sneering at my profession,
  Haven't you juggled a vast amount ?
There's the Prime Minister, in one Session,
  Juggles more games than my sins'll count.

I've murdered insects with mock thunder :
  Conscience, for that, in men don't quail.
I've made bread from the bump of wonder :
  That's my business, and there's my tale.

Fashion and rank all praised the professor:
   Ay! and I've had my smile from the Queen:
Bravo, Jerry! she meant: God bless her!
   Ain't this a sermon on that scene?

I've studied men from my topsy-turvy
   Close, and, I reckon, rather true.
Some are fine fellows: some, right scurvy:
   Most, a dash between the two.
But it's a woman, old girl, that makes me
   Think more kindly of the race,
And it's a woman, old girl, that shakes me
   When the Great Juggler I must face.

We two were married, due and legal:
   Honest we've lived since we've been one.
Lord! I could then jump like an eagle:
   You danced bright as a bit o' the sun.
Birds in a May-bush we were! right merry!
   All night we kiss'd, we juggled all day.
Joy was the heart of Juggling Jerry!
   Now from his old girl he's juggled away.

It's past parsons to console us:
   No, nor no doctor fetch for me:
I can die without my bolus;
   Two of a trade, lass, never agree!
Parson and Doctor!—don't they love rarely,
   Fighting the devil in other men's fields!
Stand up yourself and match him fairly,
   Then see how the rascal yields!

I, lass, have lived no gipsy, flaunting
   Finery while his poor helpmate grubs :
Coin I've stored, and you won't be wanting:
   You shan't beg from the troughs and tubs.
Nobly you've stuck to me, though in his kitchen
   Many a Marquis would hail you Cook !
Palaces you could have ruled and grown rich in,
   But your old Jerry you never forsook.

Hand up the chirper ! ripe ale winks in it ;
   Let's have comfort and be at peace.
Once a stout draught made me light as a linnet.
   Cheer up ! the Lord must have his lease.
Maybe—for none see in that black hollow—
   It's just a place where we're held in pawn,
And, when the Great Juggler makes as to swallow,
   It's just the sword-trick—I ain't quite gone !

Yonder came smells of the gorse, so nutty,
   Gold-like and warm : it's the prime of May.
Better than mortar, brick and putty,
   Is God's house on a blowing day.
Lean me more up the mound ; now I feel it :
   All the old heath-smells ! Ain't it strange ?
There's the world laughing, as if to conceal it,
   But He's by us, juggling the change.

I mind it well, by the sea-beach lying,
   Once—it's long gone—when two gulls we beheld,
Which, as the moon got up, were flying
   Down a big wave that sparked and swelled.

Crack went a gun : one fell : the second
  Wheeled round him twice, and was off for new luck :
There in the dark her white wing beckon'd :—
  Drop me a kiss—I'm the bird dead-struck !

George Meredith.

73. REQUIEM

UNDER the wide and starry sky,
    Dig the grave and let me lie.
Glad did I live and gladly die,
    And I laid me down with a will.

This be the verse you grave for me :
Here he lies where he longed to be ;
Home is the sailor, home from sea,
   And the hunter home from the hill.

Robert Louis Stevenson.

74. A DEAD HARVEST

In Kensington Gardens

ALONG the graceless grass of town
    They rake the rows of red and brown—
Dead leaves, unlike the rows of hay
Delicate, touched with gold and grey,
Raked long ago and far away.

A narrow silence in the park,
Between the lights a narrow dark.
One street rolls on the north ; and one,
Muffled, upon the south doth run ;
Amid the mist the work is done.

A futile crop !—for it the fire
Smoulders, and, for a stack, a pyre.
So go the town's lives on the breeze,
Even as the sheddings of the trees ;
Bosom nor barn is filled with these.

Alice Meynell.

75. THE LITTLE DANCERS

Lonely, save for a few faint stars, the sky
   Dreams ; and lonely, below, the little street
Into its gloom retires, secluded and shy.
Scarcely the dumb roar enters this soft retreat ;
And all is dark, save where come flooding rays
From a tavern window : there, to the brisk measure
Of an organ that down in an alley merrily plays,
Two children, all alone and no one by,
Holding their tattered frocks, through an airy maze
Of motion, lightly threaded with nimble feet,
Dance sedately : face to face they gaze,
Their eyes shining, grave with a perfect pleasure.

Laurence Binyon.

76. LONDON SNOW

When men were all asleep the snow came flying,
   In large white flakes falling on the city brown,
Stealthily and perpetually settling and loosely lying,
   Hushing the latest traffic of the drowsy town ;
Deadening, muffling, stifling its murmurs failing ;
Lazily and incessantly floating down and down :
   Silently sifting and veiling road, roof and railing ;

Hiding difference, making unevenness even,
Into angles and crevices softly drifting and sailing.
    All night it fell, and when full inches seven
It lay in the depth of its uncompacted lightness,
The clouds blew off from a high and frosty heaven ;
    And all woke earlier for the unaccustomed bright-
        ness
Of the winter dawning, the strange unheavenly glare :
The eye marvelled—marvelled at the dazzling white-
        ness ;
    The ear hearkened to the stillness of the solemn air ;
No sound of wheel rumbling nor of foot falling,
And the busy morning cries came thin and spare.
    Then boys I heard, as they went to school, calling,
They gathered up the crystal manna to freeze
Their tongues with tasting, their hands with snow-
        balling ;
    Or rioted in a drift, plunging up to the knees ;
Or peering up from under the white-mossed wonder,
" O look at the trees ! " they cried, " O look at the
        trees ! "
    With lessened load a few carts creak and blunder,
Following along the white deserted way,
A country company long dispersed asunder :
    When now already the sun, in pale display
Standing by Paul's high dome, spread forth below
His sparkling beams, and awoke the stir of the day.
    For now doors open, and war is waged with the
        snow ;
And trains of sombre men, past tale of number,
Tread long brown paths, as toward their toil they go ;

But even for them awhile no cares encumber
Their minds diverted ; the daily word is unspoken,
The daily thoughts of labour and sorrow slumber
At the sight of the beauty that greets them, for the
    charm they have broken.

Robert Bridges.

77. THE ROAD MENDERS

How solitary gleams the lamplit street
    Waiting the far-off morn !
How softly from the unresting city blows
The murmur borne
Down this deserted way !
Dim loiterers pass home with stealthy feet.
Now only, sudden at their interval,
The lofty chimes awaken and let fall
Deep thrills of ordered sound ;
Subsiding echoes gradually drowned
In a great stillness, that creeps up around,
And darkly grows
Profounder over all
Like a strong frost, hushing a stormy day.

But who is this, that by the brazier red
Encamped in his rude hut,
With many a sack about his shoulder spread
Watches with eyes unshut ?
The burning brazier flushes his old face,
Illumining the old thoughts in his eyes.
Surely the Night doth to her secrecies
Admit him, and the watching stars attune

To their high patience, who so lightly seems
To bear the weight of many thousand dreams
(Dark hosts around him sleeping numberless) ;
He surely hath unbuilt all walls of thought
To reach an air-wide wisdom, past access
Of us, who labour in the noisy noon,
The noon that knows him not.

For lo, at last the gloom slowly retreats,
And swiftly, like an army, comes the Day,
All bright and loud through the awakened streets
Sending a cheerful hum.
And he has stolen away.
Now, with the morning shining round them, come
Young men, and strip their coats
And loose the shirts about their throats,
And lightly up their ponderous hammers lift,
Each in his turn descending swift
With triple strokes that answer and begin
Duly, and quiver in repeated change,
Marrying the eager echoes that weave in
A music clear and strange.
But pausing soon, each lays his hammer down
And deeply breathing bares
His chest, stalwart and brown,
To the sunny airs.
Laughing one to another, limber hand
On limber hip, flushed in a group they stand,
And now untired renew their ringing toil.
The sun stands high, and ever a fresh throng
Comes murmuring ; but that eddying turmoil

Leaves many a loiterer, prosperous or unfed,
On easy or unhappy ways
At idle gaze,
Charmed in the sunshine and the rhythm enthralling,
As of unwearied Fates, for ever young,
That on the anvil of necessity
From measureless desire and quivering fear,
With musical sure lifting and downfalling
Of arm and hammer driven perpetually,
Beat out in obscure span
The fiery destiny of man.

Laurence Binyon.

78. STREET LANTERNS

COUNTRY roads are yellow and brown.
　　We mend the roads in London town.

Never a hansom dare come nigh,
Never a cart goes rolling by.

An unwonted silence steals
In between the turning wheels.

Quickly ends the autumn day,
And the workman goes his way,

Leaving, midst the traffic rude,
One small isle of solitude,

Lit, throughout the lengthy night,
By the little lantern's light.

Jewels of the dark have we,
Brighter than the rustic's be.

Over the dull earth are thrown
Topaz, and the ruby stone.

Mary E. Coleridge.

79. O SUMMER SUN

O SUMMER sun, O moving trees !
   O cheerful human noise, O busy glittering
street !
What hour shall Fate in all the future find,
Or what delights, ever to equal these :
Only to taste the warmth, the light, the wind,
Only to be alive, and feel that life is sweet ?

Laurence Binyon.

80. LONDON

ATHWART the sky a lowly sigh
   From west to east the sweet wind carried ;
The sun stood still on Primrose Hill ;
   His light in all the city tarried :
The clouds on viewless columns bloomed
Like smouldering lilies unconsumed.

" Oh sweetheart, see ! how shadowy,
   Of some occult magician's rearing,
Or swung in space of heaven's grace
   Dissolving, dimly reappearing,
Afloat upon ethereal tides
St. Paul's above the city rides ! "

A rumour broke through the thin smoke
   Enwreathing abbey, tower, and palace,
The parks, the squares, the thoroughfares,
   The million-peopled lanes and alleys,
An ever-muttering prisoned storm,
The heart of London beating warm.

John Davidson.

81. NOVEMBER BLUE

The golden tint of the electric lights seems to give a comple-
mentary colour to the air in the early evening.—*Essay on London.*

O HEAVENLY colour, London town
   Has blurred it from her skies ;
And, hooded in an earthly brown,
   Unheaven'd the city lies.
No longer standard-like this hue
   Above the broad road flies ;
Nor does the narrow street the blue
   Wear, slender pennon-wise.

But when the gold and silver lamps
   Colour the London dew,
And, misted by the winter damps,
   The shops shine bright anew—
Blue comes to earth, it walks the street,
   It dyes the wide air through ;
A mimic sky about their feet,
   The throng go crowned with blue.

Alice Meynell.

7

82. PHILOMEL IN LONDON

Not within a granite pass,
    Dim with flowers and soft with grass—
Nay, but doubly, trebly sweet
In a poplared London street,
While below my windows go
Noiseless barges, to and fro,
    Through the night's calm deep,
Ah ! what breaks the bonds of sleep ?

No steps on the pavement fall,
Soundless swings the dark canal ;
From a church-tower out of sight
Clangs the central hour of night.
Hark ! the Dorian nightingale !
Pan's voice melted to a wail !
    Such another bird
Attic Tereus never heard.

Hung above the gloom and stain—
London's squalid cope of pain—
Pure as starlight, bold as love,
Honouring our scant poplar-grove,
That most heavenly voice of earth
Thrills in passion, grief or mirth,
    Laves our poison'd air
Life's best song-bath crystal-fair.

While the starry minstrel sings
Little matters what he brings,
Be it sorrow, be it pain,
Let him sing and sing again,

Till, with dawn, poor souls rejoice,
Wakening, once to hear his voice,
 Ere afar he flies,
Bound for purer woods and skies.

 Edmund Gosse.

83. ANNUS MIRABILIS (1902)

DAYLIGHT was down, and up the cool
 Bare heaven the moon, o'er roof and elm,
Daughter of dusk most wonderful,
 Went mounting to her realm :
And night was only half begun
Round Edwardes Square in Kensington.

A Sabbath-calm possessed her face,
 An even glow her bosom filled ;
High in her solitary place
 The huntress-heart was stilled :
With bow and arrows all laid down
She stood and looked on London town.

Nay, how can sight of us give rest
 To that far-travelled heart, or draw
The musings of that tranquil breast ?
 I thought—and gazing, saw
Far up above me, high, oh, high,
From south to north a heron fly !

Oh, swiftly answered ! yonder flew
 The wings of freedom and of hope !
Little of London town he knew,
 The far horizon was his scope.

High up he sails, and sees beneath
The glimmering ponds of Hampstead Heath,

Hendon, and farther out afield
   Low water-meads are in his ken,
And lonely pools by Harrow Weald,
   And solitudes unloved of men,
Where he his fisher's spear dips down :
Little he knows of London town.

So small, with all its miles of sin,
   Is London to the grey-winged bird,
A cuckoo called at Lincoln's Inn
   Last April ; in Soho was heard
The missel-thrush with throat of glee,
And nightingales at Battersea !
Laurence Housman.

84. FLEET STREET

I NEVER see the newsboys run
   Amid the whirling street,
   With swift untiring feet,
To cry the latest venture done,
But I expect one day to hear
   Them cry the crack of doom
   And risings from the tomb,
With great Archangel Michael near ;
And see them running from the Fleet
   As messengers of God,
   With Heaven's tidings shod
About their brave unwearied feet.
Shane Leslie.

85. IN THE MEADOWS AT MANTUA

BUT to have lain upon the grass
    One perfect day, one perfect hour,
Beholding all things mortal pass
Into the quiet of green grass ;

But to have lain and loved the sun,
Under the shadow of the trees,
To have been found in unison,
Once only, with the blessed sun ;

Ah ! in these flaring London nights,
Where midnight withers into morn,
How quiet a rebuke it writes
Across the sky of London nights !

Upon the grass at Mantua
These London nights were all forgot.
They wake for me again : but ah,
The meadow-grass at Mantua !

Arthur Symons.

86. LEISURE

WHAT is this life if, full of care,
    We have no time to stand and stare.

No time to stand beneath the boughs
And stare as long as sheep or cows.

No time to see, when woods we pass,
Where squirrels hide their nuts in grass.

No time to see, in broad daylight,
Streams full of stars, like skies at night.

No time to turn at Beauty's glance,
And watch her feet, how they can dance.

No time to wait till her mouth can
Enrich that smile her eyes began.

A poor life this if, full of care,
We have no time to stand and stare.

William H. Davies.

87. LYING IN THE GRASS

BETWEEN two russet tufts of summer grass,
   I watch the world through hot air as through
   glass,
And by my face sweet lights and colours pass.

Before me, dark against the fading sky,
I watch three mowers mowing, as I lie :
With brawny arms they sweep in harmony.

Brown English faces by the sun burnt red,
Rich glowing colour on bare throat and head,
My heart would leap to watch them, were I dead !

And in my strong young living as I lie,
I seem to move with them in harmony,—
A fourth is mowing, and that fourth am I.

The music of the scythes that glide and leap,
The young men whistling as their great arms sweep,
And all the perfume and sweet sense of sleep,

The weary butterflies that droop their wings,
The dreamy nightingale that hardly sings,
And all the lassitude of happy things

Is mingling with the warm and pulsing blood
That gushes through my veins a languid flood,
And feeds my spirit as the sap a bud.

Behind the mowers, on the amber air,
A dark-green beech-wood rises, still and fair,
A white path winding up it like a stair.

And see that girl, with pitcher on her head,
And clean white apron on her gown of red,—
Her even-song of love is but half-said :

She waits the youngest mower.   Now he goes ;
Her cheeks are redder than the wild blush-rose ;
They climb up where the deepest shadows close.

But though they pass and vanish, I am there ;
I watch his rough hands meet beneath her hair,
Their broken speech sounds sweet to me like prayer

Ah ! now the rosy children come to play,
And romp and struggle with the new-mown hay ;
Their clear high voices sound from far away.

They know so little why the world is sad,
They dig themselves warm graves and yet are glad ;
Their muffled screams and laughter make me mad !

I long to go and play among them there,
Unseen, like wind, to take them by the hair,
And gently make their rosy cheeks more fair.

The happy children ! full of frank surprise,
And sudden whims and innocent ecstasies ;
What godhead sparkles from their liquid eyes !

No wonder round those urns of mingled clays
That Tuscan potters fashion'd in old days,
And coloured like the torrid earth ablaze,

We find the little gods and loves portray'd
Through ancient forests wandering undismay'd,
Or gathered, whispering, in some pleasant glade.

They knew, as I do now, what keen delight
A strong man feels to watch the tender flight
Of little children playing in his sight.

I do not hunger for a well-stored mind,
I only wish to live my life, and find
My heart in unison with all mankind.

My life is like the single dewy star
That trembles on the horizon's primrose-bar,—
A microcosm where all things living are,

And if, among the noiseless grasses, Death
Should come behind and take away my breath,
I should not rise as one who sorroweth ;

For I should pass, but all the world would be
Full of desire and young delight and glee,
And why should men be sad through loss of me ?

The light is dying ; in the silver-blue
The young moon shines from her bright window
   through :
The mowers all are gone, and I go too.

                    Edmund Gosse.

88. DOWN BY THE SALLEY GARDENS

Down by the salley gardens my love and I did
   meet ;
She passed the salley gardens with little snow-white
   feet.
She bid me take love easy, as the leaves grow on the
   tree ;
But I, being young and foolish, with her would not
   agree.

In a field by the river my love and I did stand,
And on my leaning shoulder she laid her snow-white
   hand.
She bid me take life easy, as the grass grows on the
   weirs ;
But I was young and foolish, and now am full of tears.

                    W. B. Yeats.

89. RENAISSANCE

O HAPPY soul, forget thy self !
     This that has haunted all the past,
That conjured disappointments fast,
That never could let well alone ;
That, climbing to achievement's throne,
Slipped on the last step ; this that wove
Dissatisfaction's clinging net,
And ran through life like squandered pelf :—
This that till now has been thy self
Forget, O happy soul, forget.

If ever thou didst aught commence,—
Set'st forth in springtide woods to rove,—
Or, when the sun in July throve,
Didst plunge into calm bay of ocean
With fine felicity in motion,—
Or, having climbed some high hill's brow,
Thy toil behind thee like the night,
Stoodst in the chill dawn's air intense ;—
Commence thus now, thus recommence :
Take to the future as to light.

Not as a bather on the shore
Strips of his clothes, glad soul, strip thou :
He throws them off, but folds them now ;
Although he for the billows yearns,
To weight them down with stones he turns ;
To mark the spot he scans the shore ;
Of his return he thinks before.
Do thou forget

All that, until this joy franchised thee,
Tainted thee, stained thee, or disguised thee ;
For gladness, henceforth without let,
Be thou a body, naked, fair ;
And be thy kingdom all the air
Which the noon fills with light ;
And be thine actions every one,
Like to a dawn or set of sun,
Robed in an ample glory's peace ;
Since thou hast tasted this great glee
Whose virtue prophesies in thee
That wrong is wholly doomed, is doomed and bound
  to cease.

T. Sturge Moore.

90. TO WILL. H. LOW

YOUTH now flees on feathered foot
 Faint and fainter sounds the flute,
Rarer songs of gods ; and still
Somewhere on the sunny hill,
Or along the winding stream,
Through the willows, flits a dream ;
Flits but shows a smiling face,
Flees but with so quaint a grace,
None can choose to stay at home,
All must follow, all must roam.

This is unborn beauty : she
Now in air floats high and free,
Takes the sun and breaks the blue ;—
Late with stooping pinion flew

Raking hedgerow trees, and wet
Her wing in silver streams, and set
Shining foot on temple roof :
Now again she flies aloof,
Coasting mountain clouds and kiss't
By the evening's amethyst.

In wet wood and miry lane,
Still we pant and pound in vain ;
Still with leaden foot we chase
Waning pinion, fainting face ;
Still with gray hair we stumble on,
Till, behold, the vision gone !
Where hath fleeting beauty led ?
To the doorway of the dead.
Life is over, life was gay :
We have come the primrose way.

Robert Louis Stevenson.

91. GAUDEAMUS IGITUR

COME, no more of grief and dying !
    Sing the time too swiftly flying.
        Just an hour
        Youth's in flower,
Give me roses to remember
In the shadow of December.

Fie on steeds with leaden paces !
Winds shall bear us on our races,
        Speed, O speed,
        Wind, my steed,
Beat the lightning for your master,
Yet my Fancy shall fly faster,

Give me music, give me rapture,
Youth that's fled can none recapture ;
  Not with thought
  Wisdom's bought.
Out on pride and scorn and sadness !
Give me laughter, give me gladness.

Sweetest Earth, I love and love thee,
Seas about thee, skies above thee,
  Sun and storms,
  Hues and forms
Of the clouds with floating shadows
On thy mountains and thy meadows.

Earth, there's none that can enslave thee,
Not thy lords it is that have thee ;
  Not for gold
  Art thou sold,
But thy lovers at their pleasure
Take thy beauty and thy treasure.

While sweet fancies meet me singing,
While the April blood is springing
  In my breast,
  While a jest
And my youth thou yet must leave me,
Fortune, 'tis not thou canst grieve me.

When at length the grasses cover
Me, the world's unwearied lover,
  If regret
  Haunt me yet,

It shall be for joys untasted,
Nature lent and folly wasted.

Youth and jests and summer weather,
Goods that kings and clowns together
          Waste or use
          As they choose,
These, the best, we miss pursuing
Sullen shades that mock our wooing.

Feigning Age will not delay it—
When the reckoning comes we'll pay it,
          Own our mirth
          Has been worth
All the forfeit light or heavy
Wintry Time and Fortune levy.

Feigning grief will not escape it,
What though ne'er so well you ape it—
          Age and care
          All must share,
All alike must pay hereafter,
Some for sighs and some for laughter.

Know, ye sons of Melancholy,
To be young and wise is folly.
          'Tis the weak
          Fear to wreak
On this clay of life their fancies,
Shaping battles, shaping dances.

While ye scorn our names unspoken,
Roses dead and garlands broken,
   O ye wise,
   We arise,
Out of failures, dreams, disasters,
We arise to be your masters.
Margaret L. Woods.

92. O DREAMY, GLOOMY, FRIENDLY TREES !

O DREAMY, gloomy, friendly Trees,
   I came along your narrow track
To bring my gifts unto your knees
   And gifts did you give back ;
For when I brought this heart that burns—
   These thoughts that bitterly repine—
And laid them here among the ferns
   And the hum of boughs divine,
Ye, vastest breathers of the air,
   Shook down with slow and mighty poise
Your coolness on the human care,
   Your wonder on its toys,
Your greenness on the heart's despair,
   Your darkness on its noise.
Herbert Trench.

93. IDLENESS

O IDLENESS, too fond of me,
   Begone, I know and hate thee !
Nothing canst thou of pleasure see
   In one that so doth rate thee ;

For empty are both mind and heart
   While thou with me dost linger ;
More profit would to thee impart
   A babe that sucks its finger.

I know thou hast a better way
   To spend these hours thou squand'rest ;
Some lad toils in the trough to-day
   Who groans because thou wand'rest ;

A bleating sheep he dowses now
   Or wrestles with ram's terror ;
Ah, 'mid the washing's hubbub, how
   His sighs reproach thine error !

He knows and loves thee, Idleness ;
   For when his sheep are browsing,
His open eyes enchant and bless
   A mind divinely drowsing ;

No slave to sleep, he wills and sees
   From hill-lawns the brown tillage ;
Green winding lanes and clumps of trees,
   Far town or nearer village,

The sea itself ; the fishing fleet
   Where more, thine idle lovers,
Heark'ning to sea-mews find thee sweet
   Like him who hears the plovers.

Begone ; those haul their ropes at sea,
   These plunge sheep in yon river :
Free, free from toil thy friends, and me
   From Idleness deliver !

                   T. Sturge Moore.

94. YOUTH AND LOVE

To the heart of youth the world is a highwayside.
　　Passing for ever, he fares ; and on either hand,
Deep in the gardens golden pavilions hide,
Nestle in orchard bloom, and far on the level land
Call him with lighted lamp in the eventide.

Thick as the stars at night when the moon is down,
Pleasures assail him.　He to his nobler fate
Fares ; and but waves a hand as he passes on,
Cries but a wayside word to her at the garden gate,
Sings but a boyish stave and his face is gone.

Robert Louis Stevenson.

95. THE PRECEPT OF SILENCE

I know you : solitary griefs,
　　Desolate passions, aching hours !
I know you : tremulous beliefs,
Agonised hopes, and ashen flowers !

The winds are sometimes sad to me ;
The starry spaces, full of fear :
Mine is the sorrow on the sea,
And mine the sigh of places drear.

Some players upon plaintive strings
Publish their wistfulness abroad :
I have not spoken of these things,
Save to one man, and unto God.

Lionel Johnson.

8

96. IF THIS WERE FAITH

GOD, if this were enough,
   That I see things bare to the buff
And up to the buttocks in mire ;
That I ask nor hope nor hire,
Nut in the husk,
Nor dawn beyond the dusk,
Nor life beyond death :
God, if this were faith ?

Having felt thy wind in my face
Spit sorrow and disgrace,
Having seen thine evil doom
In Golgotha and Khartoum,
And the brutes, the work of thine hands,
Fill with injustice lands
And stain with blood the sea :
If still in my veins the glee
Of the black night and the sun
And the lost battle, run :
If, an adept,
The iniquitous lists I still accept
With joy, and joy to endure and be withstood,
And still to battle and perish for a dream of good :
God, if that were enough ?

If to feel, in the ink of the slough,
And the sink of the mire,
Veins of glory and fire
Run through and transpierce and transpire,
And a secret purpose of glory in every part,

And the answering glory of battle fill my heart ;
To thrill with the joy of girded men,
To go on for ever and fail and go on again,
And be mauled to the earth and arise,
And contend for the shade of a word and a thing not
  seen with the eyes :
With the half of a broken hope for a pillow at night
That somehow the right is the right
And the smooth shall bloom from the rough :
Lord, if that were enough ?

      Robert Louis Stevenson.

97. VITAI LAMPADA

THERE's a breathless hush in the Close to-night—
 Ten to make and the match to win—
A bumping pitch and a blinding light,
 An hour to play and the last man in.
And it's not for the sake of a ribboned coat,
 Or the selfish hope of a season's fame,
But his Captain's hand on his shoulder smote
 " Play up ! play up ! and play the game ! "

The sand of the desert is sodden red,—
 Red with the wreck of a square that broke ;—
The Gatling's jammed and the Colonel dead,
 And the regiment blind with dust and smoke.
The river of death has brimmed his banks,
 And England's far, and Honour a name,
But the voice of a schoolboy rallies the ranks :
 " Play up ! play up ! and play the game ! "

This is the word that year by year,
  While in her place. the School is set,
Every one of her sons must hear,
  And none that hears it dare forget.
This they all with a joyful mind
  Bear through life like a torch in flame,
And falling fling to the host behind—
  " Play up ! play up ! and play the game ! "
                                    Henry Newbolt.

98. LAUGH AND BE MERRY

LAUGH and be merry, remember, better the world
    with a song,
Better the world with a blow in the teeth of a wrong.
Laugh, for the time is brief, a thread the length of a
    span.
Laugh, and be proud to belong to the old proud
    pageant of man.

Laugh and be merry : remember, in olden time,
God made Heaven and Earth for joy He took in a
    rhyme,
Made them, and filled them full with the strong red
    wine of His mirth,
The splendid joy of the stars : the joy of the earth.

So we must laugh and drink from the deep blue cup
    of the sky,
Join the jubilant song of the great stars sweeping by,
Laugh, and battle, and work, and drink of the wine
    outpoured
In the dear green earth, the sign of the joy of the
    Lord.

Laugh and be merry together, like brothers akin,
Guesting awhile in the rooms of a beautiful inn,
Glad till the dancing stops, and the lilt of the music
    ends.
Laugh till the game is played ; and be you merry,
    my friends.

John Masefield.

99. ROUNDABOUTS AND SWINGS

IT was early last September nigh to Framlin'am-
    on-Sea,
An' 'twas Fair-day come to-morrow, an' the time
    was after tea,
An' I met a painted caravan adown a dusty lane,
A Pharaoh with his waggons comin' jolt an' creak an'
    strain ;
A cheery cove an' sunburnt, bold o' eye and wrinkled
    up,
An' beside him on the splashboard sat a brindled
    tarrier pup,
An' a lurcher wise as Solomon an' lean as fiddle-
    strings
Was joggin' in the dust along 'is roundabouts and
    swings.

" Goo'-day," said 'e ; " Goo'-day," said I ; " an'
    'ow d'you find things go,
An' what's the chance o' millions when you runs a
    travellin' show ? "

"I find," said 'e, "things very much as 'ow I've
    always found,
For mostly they goes up and down or else goes round
    and round."
·Said 'e, "The job's the very spit o' what it always
    were,
It's bread and bacon mostly when the dog don't
    catch a 'are ;
But lookin' at it broad, an' while it ain't no merchant
    king's,
What's lost upon the roundabouts we pulls up on
    the swings ! "

"Goo' luck," said 'e ; " Goo' luck," said I ; " you've
    put it past a doubt ;
An' keep that lurcher on the road, the gamekeepers
    is out ; "
'E thumped upon the footboard an' 'e lumbered on
    again
To meet a gold-dust sunset down the owl-light in
    the lane ;
An' the moon she climbed the 'azels, while a nightjar
    seemed to spin
That Pharaoh's wisdom o'er again, 'is sooth of lose-
    and-win ;
For "up an' down an' round," said 'e, " goes all
    appointed things,
An' losses on the roundabouts means profits on the
    swings ! "

Patrick R. Chalmers.

100. THE LARK ASCENDING

HE rises and begins to round,
    He drops the silver chain of sound,
Of many links without a break,
In chirrup, whistle, slur and shake,
All intervolved and spreading wide,
Like water-dimples down a tide
Where ripple ripple overcurls
And eddy into eddy whirls ;
A press of hurried notes that run
So fleet they scarce are more than one,
Yet changeingly the trills repeat
And linger ringing while they fleet,
Sweet to the quick o' the ear, and dear
To her beyond the handmaid ear,
Who sits beside our inner springs,
Too often dry for this he brings,
Which seems the very jet of earth
At sight of sun, her music's mirth,
As up he wings the spiral stair,
A song of light, and pierces air
With fountain ardour, fountain play,
To reach the shining tops of day,
And drink in everything discerned
An ecstasy to music turned,
Impelled by what his happy bill
Disperses ; drinking, showering still,
Unthinking save that he may give
His voice the outlet, there to live
Renewed in endless notes of glee,
So thirsty of his voice is he,

For all to hear and all to know
That he is joy, awake, aglow,
The tumult of the heart to hear
Through pureness filtered crystal-clear,
And know the pleasure sprinkled bright
By simple singing of delight,
Shrill, irreflective, unrestrained,
Rapt, ringing, on the jet sustained
Without a break, without a fall,
Sweet-silvery, sheer lyrical,
Perennial, quavering up the chord
Like myriad dews of sunny sward
That trembling into fulness shine,
And sparkle dropping argentine ;
Such wooing as the ear receives
From zephyr caught in choric leaves
Of aspens when their chattering net
Is flushed to white with shivers wet ;
And such the water-spirit's chime
On mountain heights in morning's prime,
Too freshly sweet to seem excess,
Too animate to need a stress ;
But wider over many heads
The starry voice ascending spreads,
Awakening, as it waxes thin,
The best in us to him akin ;
And every face, to watch him raised,
Puts on the light of children praised,
So rich our human pleasure ripes
When sweetness on sincereness pipes,
Though nought be promised from the seas,

But only a soft-ruffling breeze
Sweep glittering on a still content,
Serenity in ravishment.

For singing till his heaven fills,
'Tis love of earth that he instils,
And ever winging up and up,
Our valley is his golden cup,
And he the wine which overflows
To lift us with him as he goes :
The woods and brooks, the sheep and kine,
He is, the hills, the human line,
The meadows green, the fallows brown,
The dreams of labour in the town ;
He sings the sap, the quickened veins ;
The wedding song of sun and rains
He is, the dance of children, thanks
Of sowers, shout of primrose-banks,
And eye of violets while they breathe ;
All these the circling song will wreathe,
And you shall hear the herb and tree,
The better heart of men shall see,
Shall feel celestially, as long
As you crave nothing save the song.

Was never voice of ours could say
Our inmost in the sweetest way,
Like yonder voice aloft, and link
All hearers in the song they drink.
Our wisdom speaks from failing blood,
Our passion is too full in flood,

We want the key of his wild note
Of truthful in a tuneful throat,
The song seraphically free
Of taint of personality,
So pure that it salutes the suns
The voice of one for millions,
In whom the millions rejoice
For giving their one spirit voice

Yet men have we, whom we revere,
Now names, and men still housing here,
Whose lives, by many a battle-dint
Defaced, and grinding wheels on flint,
Yield substance, though they sing not, sweet
For song our highest heaven to greet :
Whom heavenly singing gives us new,
Enspheres them brilliant in our blue,
From firmest base to farthest leap,
Because their love of Earth is deep,
And they are warriors in accord
With life to serve, and pass reward,
So touching purest and so heard
In the brain's reflex of yon bird :
Wherefore their soul in me or mine,
Through self-forgetfulness divine,
In them, that song aloft maintains,
To fill the sky and thrill the plains
With showerings drawn from human stores,
As he to silence nearer soars,
Extends the world at wings and dome,
More spacious making more our home,

Till lost on aerial rings
In light, and then the fancy sings.
George Meredith.

101. INTO THE TWILIGHT

OUT-WORN heart, in a time out-worn,
    Come clear of the nets of wrong and right ;
Laugh, heart, again in the gray twilight ;
Sigh, heart, again in the dew of the morn.

Your mother Eire is always young,
Dew ever shining and twilight gray ;
Though hope fall from you and love decay
Burning in fires of a slanderous tongue.

Come, heart, where hill is heaped upon hill ;
For there the mystical brotherhood
Of sun and moon and hollow and wood
And river and stream work out their will ;

And God stands winding His lonely horn ;
And time and the world are ever in flight,
And love is less kind than the gray twilight,
And hope is less dear than the dew of the morn.
W. B. Yeats.

102. BY A BIER-SIDE

THIS is a sacred city built of marvellous earth.
    Life was lived nobly here to give such beauty
birth.

Beauty was in this brain and in this eager hand :
Death is so blind and dumb Death does not under-
     stand.
Death drifts the brain with dust and soils the young
  · limbs' glory,
Death makes justice a dream, and strength a traveller's
     story.
Death drives the lovely soul to wander under the sky.
Death opens unknown doors.   It is most grand to die.

John Masefield.

103. 'TIS BUT A WEEK

'TIS but a week since down the glen
     The trampling horses came
—Half a hundred fighting men
   With all their spears aflame !
They laughed and clattered as they went,
   And round about their way
The blackbirds sang with one consent
   In the green leaves of May.

Never again shall I see them pass ;
   They'll come victorious never ;
Their spears are withered all as grass,
   Their laughter's laid for ever ;
And where they clattered as they went,
   And where their hearts were gay,
The blackbirds sing with one consent
   In the green leaves of May.

Gerald Gould.

104. I LOVE ALL BEAUTEOUS THINGS

I LOVE all beauteous things,
  I seek and adore them ;
God hath no better praise,
And man in his hasty days
  Is honoured for them.

I too will something make
  And joy in the making ;
Altho' to-morrow it seem
Like the empty words of a dream
  Remembered on waking.

Robert Bridges.

105. ALL FLESH

I DO not need the skies'
  Pomp, when I would be wise ;
For pleasaunce nor to use
Heaven's champaign when I muse.
One grass-blade in its veins
Wisdom's whole flood contains :
Thereon my foundering mind
Odyssean fate can find.

O little blade, now vaunt
Thee, and be arrogant !
Tell the proud sun that he
Sweated in shaping thee ;
Night, that she did unvest
Her mooned and argent breast
To suckle thee.   Heaven fain

Yearned over thee in rain,
And with wide parent wing
Shadowed thee, nested thing,
Fed thee, and slaved for thy
Impotent tyranny.
Nature's broad thews bent
Meek for thy content.
Mastering littleness
Which the wise heavens confess,
The frailty which doth draw
Magnipotence to its law—
These were, O happy one, these
Thy laughing puissances !

Be confident of thought,
Seeing that thou art naught ;
And be thy pride thou'rt all
Delectably safe and small.
Epitomized in thee
Was the mystery
Which shakes the spheres conjoint—
God focussed to a point.

All thy fine mouths shout
Scorn upon dull-eyed doubt.
Impenetrable fool
Is he thou canst not school
To the humility
By which the angels see !
Unfathomably framed
Sister, I am not shamed

Before the cherubin
To vaunt my flesh thy kin.
My one hand thine, and one
Imprisoned in God's own,
I am as God ; alas,
And such a god of grass !
A little root clay-caught,
A wind, a flame, a thought,
Inestimably naught !

Francis Thompson.

106. TO A SNOWFLAKE

WHAT heart could have thought you ?—
    Past our devisal
(O filigree petal !)
Fashioned so purely,
Fragilely, surely,
From what Paradisal
Imagineless metal,
Too costly for cost ?
Who hammered you, wrought you,
From argentine vapour ?—
" God was my shaper.
Passing surmisal,
He hammered, He wrought me,
From curled silver vapour,
To lust of His mind :—
Thou couldst not have thought me !
So purely, so palely,
Tinily, surely,
Mightily, frailly,

Insculped and embossed,
With His hammer of wind,
And His graver of frost."

Francis Thompson.

107. TO A DAISY

SLIGHT as thou art, thou art enough to hide,
   Like all created things, secrets from me,
   And stand a barrier to eternity.
And I, how can I praise thee well and wide

From where I dwell—upon the hither side ?
   Thou little veil for so great mystery,
   When shall I penetrate all things and thee,
And then look back ?   For this I must abide,

Till thou shalt grow and fold and be unfurled
Literally between me and the world.
   Then I shall drink from in beneath a spring,

And from a poet's side shall read his book.
O daisy mine, what will it be to look
   From God's side even of such a simple thing ?

Alice Meynell.

108. LUCIFER IN STARLIGHT

ON a starred night Prince Lucifer uprose.
   Tired of his dark dominion swung the fiend
Above the rolling ball in cloud part screened,
Where sinners hugged their spectre of repose.

Poor prey to his hot fit of pride were those.
And now upon his western wing he leaned,
Now his huge bulk o'er Afric's sands careened,
Now the black planet shadowed Arctic snows.
Soaring through wider zones that pricked his scars
With memory of the old revolt from Awe,
He reached a middle height, and at the stars,
Which are the brain of heaven, he looked, and sank.
Around the ancient track marched rank on rank,
The army of unalterable law.

George Meredith.

109. THE CELESTIAL SURGEON

IF I have faltered more or less
   In my great task of happiness ;
If I have moved among my race
And shown no glorious morning face ;
If beams from happy human eyes
Have moved me not ; if morning skies,
Books, and my food, and summer rain
Knocked on my sullen heart in vain :—
Lord, thy most pointed pleasure take
And stab my spirit broad awake ;
Or, Lord, if too obdurate I,
Choose thou, before that spirit die,
A piercing pain, a killing sin,
And to my dead heart run them in !

Robert Louis Stevenson.

9

110. THE KINGDOM OF GOD
'In no Strange Land'

O WORLD invisible, we view thee,
   O world intangible, we touch thee,
O world unknowable, we know thee,
Inapprehensible, we clutch thee !

Does the fish soar to find the ocean,
   The eagle plunge to find the air—
That we ask of the stars in motion
   If they have rumour of thee there ?

Not where the wheeling systems darken,
   And our benumbed conceiving soars !—
The drift of pinions, would we hearken,
   Beats at our own clay-shuttered doors.

The angels keep their ancient places ;—
   Turn but a stone, and start a wing !
'Tis ye, 'tis your estrangèd faces,
   That miss the many-splendoured thing.

But (when so sad thou canst not sadder)
   Cry ;—and upon thy so sore loss
Shall shine the traffic of Jacob's ladder
   Pitched betwixt Heaven and Charing Cross.

Yea, in the night, my Soul, my daughter,
   Cry,—clinging Heaven by the hems ;
And lo, Christ walking on the water
   Not of Gennesareth, but Thames !
          Francis Thompson.

111. THE LADY POVERTY

THE Lady Poverty was fair :
　　But she has lost her looks of late,
With change of times and change of air.
Ah slattern ! she neglects her hair,
Her gown, her shoes ; she keeps no state
As once when her pure feet were bare.

Or—almost worse, if worse can be—
She scolds in parlours, dusts and trims,
Watches and counts.　Oh, is this she
Whom Francis met, whose step was free,
Who with Obedience carolled hymns,
In Umbria walked with Chastity ?

Where is her ladyhood ?　Not here,
Not among modern kinds of men ;
But in the stony fields, where clear
Through the thin trees the skies appear,
In delicate spare soil and fen,
And slender landscape and austere.

　　　　　　　　　Alice Meynell.

112. COURTESY

OF Courtesy it is much less
　　Than Courage of Heart or Holiness,
Yet in my Walks it seems to me
That the Grace of God is in Courtesy.

On Monks I did in Storrington fall,
They took me straight into their Hall ;
I saw Three Pictures on a wall,
And Courtesy was in them all.

The first the Annunciation;
The second the Visitation;
The third the Consolation,
Of God that was Our Lady's Son.

The first was of Saint Gabriel;
On Wings a-flame from Heaven he fell;
And as he went upon one knee
He shone with Heavenly Courtesy.

Our Lady out of Nazareth rode—
It was her month of heavy load;
Yet was Her face both great and kind,
For Courtesy was in Her Mind.

The third, it was our Little Lord,
Whom all the Kings in arms adored;
He was so small you could not see
His large intent of Courtesy.

Our Lord, that was Our Lady's Son,
Go bless you, People, one by one;
My Rhyme is written, my work is done.

Hilaire Belloc.

113. MONTSERRAT

PEACE waits among the hills;
I have drunk peace,
Here, where the blue air fills
The great cup of the hills,
And fills with peace.

Between the earth and sky,
I have seen the earth
Like a dark cloud go by,
And fade out of the sky ;
There was no more earth.

Here, where the Holy Graal
Brought secret light
Once, from beyond the veil,
I, seeing no Holy Graal,
See divine light.

Light fills the hills with God,
Wind with his breath,
And here, in his abode,
Light, wind, and air praise God,
And this poor breath.

Arthur Symons.

114. PRAYERS

GOD who created me
Nimble and light of limb,
In three elements free,
To run, to ride, to swim :
Not when the sense is dim,
But now from the heart of joy,
I would remember Him :
Take the thanks of a boy.

Jesu, King and Lord,
Whose are my foes to fight,

Gird me with Thy sword,
  Swift and sharp and bright.
Thee would I serve if I might ;
  And conquer if I can,
From day-dawn till night,
  Take the strength of a man.

Spirit of Love and Truth,
  Breathing in grosser clay,
The light and flame of youth,
  Delight of men in the fray,
Wisdom in strength's decay ;
  From pain, strife, wrong to be free,
This best gift I pray,
  Take my spirit to Thee.

Henry Charles Beeching.

115. THE SHEPHERDESS

SHE walks—the lady of my delight—
  A shepherdess of sheep.
Her flocks are thoughts.   She keeps them white ;
  She guards them from the steep ;
She feeds them on the fragrant height,
  And folds them in for sleep.

She roams maternal hills and bright,
  Dark valleys safe and deep.
Into that tender breast at night
  The chastest stars may peep.
She walks—the lady of my delight—
  A shepherdess of sheep.

She holds her little thoughts in sight,
  Though gay they run and leap.
She is so circumspect and right ;
  She has her soul to keep.
She walks—the lady of my delight—
  A shepherdess of sheep.

                              Alice Meynell.

116. GIBBERISH

MANY a flower have I seen blossom,
  Many a bird for me will sing.
Never heard I so sweet a singer,
  Never saw I so fair a thing.

She is a bird, a bird that blossoms,
  She is a flower, a flower that sings ;
And I a flower when I behold her,
  And when I hear her, I have wings.

                              Mary E. Coleridge.

117. MARTHA

" ONCE . . . once upon a time . . . "
    Over and over again,
Martha would tell us her stories,
  In the hazel glen.

Hers were those clear grey eyes
  You watch, and the story seems
Told by their beautifulness
  Tranquil as dreams.

She'd sit with her two slim hands
  Clasped round her bended knees ;
While we on our elbows lolled,
  And stared at ease.

Her voice and her narrow chin,
  Her grave small lovely head,
Seemed half the meaning
  Of the words she said.

" Once . . . once upon a time . . . "
  Like a dream you dream in the night,
Fairies and gnomes stole out
  In the leaf-green light.

And her beauty far away
  Would fade, as her voice ran on,
Till hazel and summer sun
  And all were gone :—

All fordone and forgot ;
  And like clouds in the height of the sky,
Our hearts stood still in the hush
  Of an age gone by.

                    Walter de la Mare.

118. A FRIEND

ALL, that he came to give,
    He gave, and went again :
I have seen one man live,
I have seen one man reign,
With all the graces in his train.

As one of us, he wrought
Things of the common hour :
Whence was the charmed soul brought,
That gave each act such power ;
The natural beauty of a flower ?

Magnificence and grace,
Excellent courtesy :
A brightness on the face,
Airs of high memory :
Whence came all these, to such as he ?

Like young Shakespearian kings,
He won the adoring throng :
And, as Apollo sings,
He triumphed with a song :
Triumphed, and sang, and passed along.

With a light word, he took
The hearts of men in thrall :
And, with a golden look,
Welcomed them, at his call
Giving their love, their strength, their all.

No man less proud than he,
Nor cared for homage less :
Only, he could not be
Far off from happiness :
Nature was bound to his success.

Weary, the cares, the jars,
The lets, of every day,
But the heavens filled with stars,
Chanced he upon the way :
And where he stayed, all joy would stay.

Now, when sad night draws down,
When the austere stars burn :
Roaming the vast live town,
My thoughts and memories yearn
Toward him, who never will return.

Yet have I seen him live,
And owned my friend, a king :
All that he came to give
He gave : and I, who sing
His praise, bring all I have to bring.

Lionel Johnson.

119. TWILIGHT

TWILIGHT it is, and the far woods are dim, and the
rooks cry and call.
Down in the valley the lamps, and the mist, and a
star over all,
There by the rick, where they thresh, is the drone at
an end,
Twilight it is, and I travel the road with my friend.

I think of the friends who are dead, who were dear
long ago in the past,
Beautiful friends who are dead, though I know that
death cannot last ;

Friends with the beautiful eyes that the dust has
 defiled,
Beautiful souls who were gentle when I was a child.
John Masefield.

120. ON THE DEATH OF ARNOLD TOYNBEE

GOOD-BYE ; no tears nor cries
 Are fitting here, and long lament were vain.
Only the last low words be softly said,
And the last greeting given above the dead ;
For soul more pure and beautiful our eyes
 Never shall see again.

 Alas ! what help is it,
What consolation in this heavy chance,
 That to the blameless life so soon laid low
 This was the end appointed long ago,
This the allotted space, the measure fit
 Of endless ordinance ?

 Thus were the ancient days
Made like our own monotonous with grief ;
 From unassuagèd lips even thus hath flown
 Perpetually the immemorial moan
Of those that weeping went on desolate ways,
 Nor found in tears relief.

 For faces yet grow pale,
Tears rise at fortune, and true hearts take fire
 In all who hear, with quickening pulse's stroke,
 That cry that from the infinite people broke,
When third among them Helen led the wail
 At Hector's funeral pyre.

And by the Latin beach
At rise of dawn such piteous tears were shed,   ·
  When Troy and Arcady in long array
  Followed the princely body on its way,
And Lord Aeneas spoke the last sad speech
  Above young Pallas dead.

    Even in this English clime
The same sweet cry no circling seas can drown,
  In melancholy cadence rose to swell
  Some dirge of Lycidas or Astrophel
When lovely souls and pure before their time
  Into the dusk went down.

    These Earth, the bounteous nurse,
Hath long ago lapped in deep peace divine.
  Lips that made musical their old-world woe
  Themselves have gone to silence long ago,
And left a weaker voice and wearier verse,
  O royal soul, for thine.

    Beyond our life how far
Soars his new life through radiant orb and zone,
  While we in impotency of the night
  Walk dumbly, and the path is hard, and light
Fails, and for sun and moon the single star
  Honour is left alone.

    The star that knows no set,
But circles ever with a fixed desire,
  Watching Orion's armour all of gold ;
  Watching and wearying not, till pale and cold
Dawn breaks, and the first shafts of morning fret
  The east with lines of fire.

But on the broad low plain
When night is clear and windy, with hard frost,
 Such as had once the morning in their eyes,
 Watching and wearying, gaze upon the skies,
And cannot see that star for their great pain
 Because the sun is lost.

 Alas, how all our love
Is scant at best to fill so ample room !
 Image and influence fall too fast away
 And fading memory cries at dusk of day
Deem'st thou the dust recks aught at all thereof,
 The ghost within the tomb ?

 For even o'er lives like his
The slumberous river washes soft and slow ;
 The lapping water rises wearily,
 Numbing the nerve and will to sleep ; and we
Before the goal and crown of mysteries
 Fall back, and dare not know.

 Only at times we know,
In gyres convolved and luminous orbits whirled
 The soul beyond her knowing seems to sweep
 Out of the deep, fire-winged, into the deep ;
As two, who loved each other here below
 Better than all the world,

 Yet ever held apart,
And never knew their own hearts' deepest things,
 After long lapse of periods, wandering far
 Beyond the pathways of the furthest star,
Into communicable space might dart
 With tremor of thunderous wings ;

Across the void might call
Each unto each past worlds that raced and ran,
    And flash through galaxies, and clasp and kiss
    In some slant chasm and infinite abyss
Far in the faint sidereal interval
    Between the Lyre and Swan.

J. W. Mackail.

121. ESTRANGEMENT

So, without overt breach, we fall apart,
    Tacitly sunder—neither you nor I
Conscious of one intelligible Why,
And both, from severance, winning equal smart.
So, with resigned and acquiescent heart,
Whene'er your name on some chance lip may lie,
I seem to see an alien shade pass by,
A spirit wherein I have no lot or part.

Thus may a captive, in some fortress grim,
From casual speech betwixt his warders, learn
That June on her triumphant progress goes
Through arched and bannered woodlands; while for
    him
She is a legend emptied of concern,
And idle is the rumour of the rose.

William Watson.

122. FATHERHOOD

A kiss, a word of thanks, away
    They're gone, and you forsaken learn
The blessedness of giving; they
    (So Nature bids) forget, nor turn
    To where you sit, and watch, and yearn.

And you (so Nature bids) would go
  Through fire and water for their sake ;
Rise early, late take rest, to sow
  Their wealth, and lie all night awake
  If but their little finger ache.

The storied prince with wondrous hair
  Which stole men's hearts and wrought his bale,
Rebelling, since he had no heir,
  Built him a pillar in the vale,
  —Absalom's—lest his name should fail.

It fails not, though the pillar lies
  In dust, because the outraged one,
His father, with strong agonies
  Cried it until the day was done—
  " O Absalom, my son, my son ! "

So Nature bade ; or might it be
  God, who in Jewry once (they say)
Cried with a great cry, " Come to me,
  Children," who still held on their way,
  Though He spread out His hands all day ?

                          Henry Charles Beeching.

123. DAISY

WHERE the thistle lifts a purple crown
    Six foot out of the turf,
And the harebell shakes on the windy hill—
  O the breath of the distant surf !—

The hills look over on the South,
　　And southward dreams the sea ;
And with the sea-breeze hand in hand
　　Came innocence and she.

Where 'mid the gorse the raspberry
　　Red for the gatherer springs,
Two children did we stray and talk
　　Wise, idle, childish things.

She listened with big-lipped surprise,
　　Breast-deep 'mid flower and spine :
Her skin was like a grape, whose veins
　　Run snow instead of wine.

She knew not those sweet words she spake,
　　Nor knew her own sweet way ;
But there's never a bird, so sweet a song
　　Thronged in whose throat that day.

Oh, there were flowers in Storrington
　　On the turf and on the spray ;
But the sweetest flower on Sussex hills
　　Was the Daisy-flower that day !

Her beauty smoothed earth's furrowed face ;
　　She gave me tokens three :—
A look, a word of her winsome mouth,
　　And a wild raspberry.

A berry red, a guileless look,
　　A still word,—strings of sand !
And yet they made my wild, wild heart
　　Fly down to her little hand.

For standing artless as the air,
 And candid as the skies,
She took the berries with her hand,
 And the love with her sweet eyes.

The fairest things have fleetest end,
 Their scent survives their close :
But the rose's scent is bitterness
 To him that loved the rose.

She looked a little wistfully,
 Then went her sunshine way :—
The sea's eye had a mist on it,
 And the leaves fell from the day.

She went her unremembering way,
 She went and left in me
The pang of all the partings gone,
 And partings yet to be.

She left me marvelling why my soul .
 Was sad that she was glad ;
At all the sadness in the sweet,
 The sweetness in the sad.

Still, still I seemed to see her, still
 Look up with soft replies,
And take the berries with her hand,
 And the love with her lovely eyes.

10

Nothing begins, and nothing ends,
    That is not paid with moan ;
For we are born in other's pain,
    And perish in our own.

Francis Thompson.

124. A CRADLE SONG

O, MEN from the fields !
    Come gently within.
Tread softly, softly,
    O ! men coming in.

Mavourneen is going
    From me and from you,
Where Mary will fold him
    With mantle of blue !

From reek of the smoke
    And cold of the floor,
And the peering of things
    Across the half-door.

O, men from the fields !
    Soft, softly come thro'.
Mary puts round him
    Her mantle of blue.

Padraic Colum.

125. ON A DEAD CHILD

PERFECT little body, without fault or stain on thee,
    With promise of strength and manhood full
and fair !

Though cold and stark and bare,
The bloom and the charm of life doth awhile remain
    on thee.

Thy mother's treasure wert thou ;—alas ! no longer
    To visit her heart with wondrous joy ; to be
        Thy father's pride ;—ah, he
Must gather his faith together, and his strength make
    stronger.

To me, as I move thee now in the last duty,
    Dost thou with a turn or gesture anon respond ;
        Startling my fancy fond
With a chance attitude of the head, a freak of beauty.

Thy hand clasps, as 'twas wont, my finger, and
    holds it :
    But the grasp is the clasp of Death, heartbreaking
    and stiff ;
        Yet feels to my hand as if
'Twas still thy will, thy pleasure and trust that
    enfolds it.

So I lay thee there, thy sunken eyelids closing,—
    Go, lie thou there in thy coffin, thy last little bed !—
        Propping thy wise, sad head,
Thy firm, pale hands across thy chest disposing.

So quiet ! doth the change content thee ?—Death,
    whither hath he taken thee ?
    To a world, do I think, that rights the disaster of
    this ?

The vision of which I miss,
Who weep for the body, and wish but to warm thee
and awaken thee ?

Ah ! little at best can all our hopes avail us
    To lift this sorrow, or cheer us, when in the dark,
        Unwilling, alone we embark,
And the things we have seen and have known and
    have heard of, fail us.

                                        Robert Bridges.

126. I NEVER SHALL LOVE THE SNOW AGAIN

I NEVER shall love the snow again
    Since Maurice died :
With corniced drift it blocked the lane,
· And sheeted in a desolate plain
    The country side.

The trees with silvery rime bedight
    Their branches bare.
By day no sun appeared ; by night
The hidden moon shed thievish light
    In the misty air.

We fed the birds that flew around
    In flocks to be fed :
No shelter in holly or brake they found.
The speckled thrush on the frozen ground
    Lay frozen and dead.

We skated on stream and pond ; we cut
    The crinching snow
To Doric temple or Arctic hut ;
We laughed and sang at nightfall, shut
    By the fireside glow. .

Yet grudged we our keen delights before
    Maurice should come.
We said, " In-door or out-of-door
We shall love life for a month or more,
    When he is home."

They brought him home ; 'twas two days late
    For Christmas Day :
Wrapped in white, in solemn state,
A flower in his hand, all still and straight
    Our Maurice lay.

And two days ere the year outgave
    We laid him low.
The best of us truly were not brave,
When we laid Maurice down in his grave
    Under the snow.
                 Robert Bridges.

127. TO MY GODCHILD

Francis M. W. M.

THIS labouring, vast, Tellurian galleon,
    Riding at anchor off the orient sun,
Had broken its cable, and stood out to space
Down some frore Arctic of the aërial ways :

And now, back warping from the inclement main,
Its vaporous shroudage drenched with icy rain,
It swung into its azure roads again ;
When, floated on the prosperous sun-gale, you
Lit, a white halcyon auspice, 'mid our frozen crew.

To the Sun, stranger, surely you belong,
Giver of golden days and golden song ;
Nor is it by an all-unhappy plan
You bear the name of me, his constant Magian.
Yet ah ! from any other that it came,
Lest fated to my fate you be, as to my name.
When at the first those tidings did they bring,
My heart turned troubled at the ominous thing :
Though well may such a title him endower,
For whom a poet's prayer implores a poet's power.
The Assisian, who kept plighted faith to three,
To Song, to Sanctitude, and Poverty,
(In two alone of whom most singers prove
A fatal faithfulness of during love !)
He the sweet Sales, of whom we scarcely ken
How God he could love more, he so loved men ;
The crown and crowned of Laura and Italy ;
And Fletcher's fellow—from these, and not from me,
Take you your name, and take your legacy !

Or, if a right successive you declare
When worms, for ivies, intertwine my hair,
Take but this Poesy that now followeth
My clayey hest with sullen servile breath,
Made then your happy freedman by testating death.

My song I do but hold for you in trust,
I ask you but to blossom from my dust.
When you have compassed all weak I began,
Diviner poet, and ah ! diviner man ;
The man at feud with the perduring child
In you before Song's altar nobly reconciled ;
From the wise heavens I half shall smile to see
How little a world, which owned you, needed me.
If, while you keep the vigils of the night,
For your wild tears make darkness all too bright,
Some lone orb through your lonely window peeps,
As it played lover over your sweet sleeps ;
Think it a golden crevice in the sky,
Which I have pierced but to behold you by !

And when, immortal mortal, droops your head,
And you, the child of deathless song, are dead ;
Then, as you search with unaccustomed glance
The ranks of Paradise for my countenance,
Turn not your tread along the Uranian sod
Among the bearded counsellors of God ;
For if in Eden as on earth are we,
I sure shall keep a younger company :
Pass where beneath their rangèd gonfalons
The starry cohorts shake their shielded suns,
The dreadful mass of their enridgèd spears ;
Pass where majestical the eternal peers,
The stately choice of the great Saintdom, meet—
A silvern segregation, globed complete
In sandalled shadow of the Triune feet ;
Pass by where wait, young poet-wayfarer,

Your cousined clusters, emulous to share
With you the roseal lightnings burning 'mid their
 hair ;
Pass the crystalline sea, the Lampads seven :—
Look for me in the nurseries of Heaven.
Francis Thompson.

128. WHEN JUNE IS COME

WHEN June is come, then all the day
  I'll sit with my love in the scented hay :
And watch the sunshot palaces high,
That the white clouds build in the breezy sky.

She singeth, and I do make her a song,
And read sweet poems the whole day long :
Unseen as we lie in our hay-built home.
Oh, life is delight when June is come.
Robert Bridges.

129. IN MISTY BLUE

IN misty blue the lark is heard
  Above the silent homes of men ;
The bright-eyed thrush, the little wren,
The yellow-billed sweet-voiced blackbird
Mid sallow blossoms blond as curd
Or silver oak boughs, carolling
With happy throat from tree to tree,
Sing into light this morn of spring
That sang my dear love home to me.

Be starry, buds of clustered white,
Around the dark waves of her hair !
The young fresh glory you prepare
Is like my ever-fresh delight
When she comes shining on my sight
With meeting eyes, with such a cheek
As colours fair like flushing tips
Of shoots, and music ere she speak
Lies in the wonder of her lips.

Airs of the morning, breathe about
Keen faint scents of the wild wood side
From thickets where primroses hide
Mid the brown leaves of winter's rout.
Chestnut and willow, beacon out
For joy of her, from far and nigh,
Your English green on English hills :
Above her head, song-quivering sky,
And at her feet, the daffodils.

Because she breathed, the world was more,
And breath a finer soul to use,
And life held lovelier hopes to choose :
But O, to-day my heart brims o'er,
Earth glows as from a kindled core,
Like shadows of diviner things
Are hill and cloud and flower and tree—
A splendour that is hers and spring's,—
The day my love came home to me.

Laurence Binyon.

130. IN FOUNTAIN COURT

THE fountain murmuring of sleep,
 A drowsy tune ;
The flickering green of leaves that keep
 The light of June ;
Peace, through a slumbering afternoon,
 The peace of June.

A waiting ghost, in the blue sky,
 The white curved moon ;
June, hushed and breathless, waits, and I
 Wait, too, with June ;
Come, through the lingering afternoon,
 Soon, love, come soon.

Arthur Symons.

131. THE PRAISE OF DUST

" WHAT of vile dust ? " the preacher said.
 Methought the whole world woke,
The dead stone lived beneath my foot,
 And my whole body spoke.

" You that play tyrant to the dust,
 And stamp its wrinkled face,
This patient star that flings you not
 Far into homeless space,

" Come down out of your dusty shrine
 The living dust to see,
The flowers that at your sermon's end
 Stand blazing silently,

" Rich white and blood-red blossom ; stones,
   Lichens like fire encrust ;
A gleam of blue, a glare of gold,
   The vision of the dust.

" Pass them all by ; till, as you come
   Where, at a city's edge,
Under a tree—I know it well—
   Under a lattice ledge,

" The sunshine falls on one brown head.
   You, too, O cold of clay,
Eater of stones, may haply hear
   The trumpets of that day

" When God to all his paladins
   By his own splendour swore
To make a fairer face than heaven,
   Of dust and nothing more."

                                 G. K. Chesterton.

132. AWAKE, MY HEART, TO BE LOVED

AWAKE, my heart, to be loved, awake, awake !
   The darkness silvers away, the morn doth
break,
It leaps in the sky : unrisen lustres slake
The o'ertaken moon.   Awake, O heart, awake !

She too that loveth awaketh and hopes for thee ;
Her eyes already have sped the shades that flee,

Already they watch the path thy feet shall take :
Awake, O heart, to be loved, awake, awake !

And if thou tarry from her,—if this could be,—
She cometh herself, O heart, to be loved, to thee ;
For thee would unashamèd herself forsake :
Awake to be loved, my heart, awake, awake !

Awake ! the land is scattered with light, and see,
Uncanopied sleep is flying from field and tree :
And blossoming boughs of April in laughter shake ;
Awake, O heart, to be loved, awake, awake !

Lo all things wake and tarry and look for thee :
She looketh and saith, " O sun, now bring him to me.
Come more adored, O adored, for his coming's sake,
And awake my heart to be loved : awake, awake ! "

Robert Bridges.

133. AEDH WISHES FOR THE CLOTHS OF HEAVEN

HAD I the heavens' embroidered cloths,
    Enwrought with golden and silver light,
The blue and the dim and the dark cloths
Of night and light and the half light,
I would spread the cloths under your feet :
But I, being poor, have only my dreams ;
I have spread my dreams under your feet ;
Tread softly because you tread on my dreams.

W. B. Yeats.

134. BEAUTY

I HAVE seen dawn and sunset on moors and windy
    hills
Coming in solemn beauty like slow old tunes of Spain :
I have seen the lady April bringing the daffodils,
Bringing the springing grass and the soft warm April
    rain.

I have heard the song of the blossoms and the old
    chant of the sea,
And seen strange lands from under the arched white
    sails of ships ;
But the loveliest things of beauty God ever has
    showed to me,
Are her voice, and her hair, and eyes, and the dear red
    curve of her lips.

John Masefield.

135. MY WIFE

TRUSTY, dusky, vivid, true,
    With eyes of gold and bramble-dew,
Steel-true and blade-straight,
The great artificer
Made my mate.

Honour, anger, valour, fire ;
A love that life could never tire,
Death quench or evil stir,
The mighty master
Gave to her.

Teacher, tender, comrade, wife,
A fellow-farer true through life,
Heart-whole and soul-free
The august father
Gave to me.

Robert Louis Stevenson.

136. FROM "LOVE IN THE VALLEY"

SHY as the squirrel and wayward as the swallow,
   Swift as the swallow along the river's light
Circleting the surface to meet his mirrored winglets,
   Fleeter she seems in her stay than in her flight.
Shy as the squirrel that leaps among the pine-tops,
   Wayward as the swallow overhead at set of sun,
She whom I love is hard to catch and conquer,
   Hard, but O the glory of the winning were she won !
      *   *   *   *   *
Heartless she is as the shadow in the meadows
   Flying to the hills on a blue and breezy noon.
No, she is athirst and drinking up her wonder :
   Earth to her is young as the slip of the new moon.
Deals she an unkindness, 'tis but her rapid measure,
   Even as in a dance ; and her smile can heal no less :
Like the swinging May-cloud that pelts the flowers
    with hailstones
   Off a sunny border, she was made to bruise and
    bless.
      *   *   *   *   *
Stepping down the hill with her fair companions,
   Arm in arm, all against the raying West,

Boldly she sings, to the merry tune she marches,
　Brave is her shape, and sweeter unpossessed.
Sweeter, for she is what my heart first awaking
　Whispered the world was ; morning light is she.
Love that so desires would fain keep her changeless ;
　Fain would fling the net, and fain have her free.

　　　　*　　*　　*　　*　　*

Happy, happy time, when the white star hovers
　Low over dim fields fresh with bloomy dew,
Near the face of dawn, that draws athwart the dark-
　　ness,
　Threading it with colour, like yewberries the yew.
Thicker crowd the shades as the grave East deepens,
　Glowing, and with crimson a long cloud swells.
Maiden still the morn is ; and strange she is, and
　　secret ;
　Strange her eyes ; her cheeks are cold as cold sea-
　　shells.

　　　　*　　*　　*　　*　　*

Peering at her chamber the white crowns the red rose,
　Jasmine winds the porch with stars two and three.
Parted is the window ; she sleeps ; the starry jasmine
　Breathes a falling breath that carries thoughts of
　　me.
Sweeter unpossessed, have I said of her my sweetest ?
　Not while she sleeps : while she sleeps the jasmine
　　breathes,
Luring her to love ; she sleeps ; the starry jasmine
　Bears me to her pillow under white rose-wreaths.

　　　　　　　　　　George Meredith.

137. TO THE BELOVED

OH, not more subtly silence strays
    Amongst the winds, between the voices,
Mingling alike with pensive lays,
    And with the music that rejoices,
Than thou art present in my days.

My silence, life returns to thee
    In all the pauses of her breath.
Hush back to rest the melody
    That out of thee awakeneth ;
And thou, wake ever, wake for me !

Thou art like silence all unvexed,
    Though wild words part my soul from thee.
Thou art like silence unperplexed,
    A secret and a mystery
Between one footfall and the next.

Most dear pause in a mellow lay !
    Thou art inwoven with every air.
With thee the wildest tempests play,
    And snatches of thee everywhere
Make little heavens throughout a day.

Darkness and solitude shine, for me.
    For life's fair outward part are rife
The silver noises ; let them be.
    It is the very soul of life
Listens for thee, listens for thee.

O pause between the sobs of cares ;
  O thought within all thought that is ;
Trance between laughters unawares :
  Thou art the shape of melodies,
And thou the ecstasy of prayers !

Alice Meynell.

138. WHEN YOU ARE OLD

WHEN you are old and gray and full of sleep,
  And nodding by the fire, take down this book,
And slowly read, and dream of the soft look
Your eyes had once, and of their shadows deep ;

How many loved your moments of glad grace,
And loved your beauty with love false or true ;
But one man loved the pilgrim soul in you,
And loved the sorrows of your changing face.

And bending down beside the glowing bars
Murmur, a little sadly, how love fled
And paced upon the mountains overhead
And hid his face amid a crowd of stars.

W. B. Yeats.

139. I WILL NOT LET THEE GO

I WILL not let thee go.
  Ends all our month-long love in this ?
  Can it be summed up so,
  Quit in a single kiss ?
  I will not let thee go.

I will not let thee go.
If thy words' breath could scare thy deeds,
    As the soft south can blow
    And toss the feathered seeds,
    Then might I let thee go.

    I will not let thee go.
Had not the great sun seen, I might ;
    Or were he reckoned slow
    To bring the false to light,
    Then might I let thee go.

    I will not let thee go.
The stars that crowd the summer skies
    Have watched us so below
    With all their million eyes,
    I dare not let thee go.

    I will not let thee go.
Have we not chid the changeful moon,
    Now rising late, and now
    Because she set too soon,
    And shall I let thee go ?

    I will not let thee go.
Have not the young flowers been content,
    Plucked ere their buds could blow,
    To seal our sacrament ?
    I cannot let thee go.

I will not let thee go.
I hold thee by too many bands :
Thou sayest farewell, and lo !
I have thee by the hands,
And will not let thee go.

Robert Bridges.

140. PARTED

FAREWELL to one now silenced quite,
Sent out of hearing, out of sight,—
My friend of friends, whom I shall miss.
He is not banished, though, for this,—
Nor he, nor sadness, nor delight.

Though I shall talk with him no more,
A low voice sounds upon the shore.
He must not watch my resting-place,
But who shall drive a mournful face
From the sad winds about my door ?

I shall not hear his voice complain,
But who shall stop the patient rain ?
His tears must not disturb my heart,
But who shall change the years, and part
The world from every thought of pain ?

Although my life is left so dim,
The morning crowns the mountain-rim ;
Joy is not gone from summer skies,
Nor innocence from children's eyes,
And all these things are part of him

He is not banished, for the showers
Yet wake this green warm earth of ours.
How can the summer but be sweet ?
I shall not have him at my feet,
And yet my feet are on the flowers.

Alice Meynell.

141. ELEGY ON A LADY, WHOM GRIEF FOR THE DEATH OF HER BETROTHED KILLED

ASSEMBLE, all ye maidens, at the door,
And all ye loves, assemble ; far and wide
Proclaim the bridal, that proclaimed before
Has been deferred to this late eventide :
For on this night the bride,
The days of her betrothal over,
Leaves the parental hearth for evermore ;
To-night the bride goes forth to meet her lover.

Reach down the wedding vesture, that has lain
Yet all unvisited, the silken gown :
Bring out the bracelets, and the golden chain
Her dearer friends provided : sere and brown
Bring out the festal crown,
And set it on her forehead lightly :
Though it be withered, twine no wreath again ;
This only is the crown she can wear rightly.

Cloak her in ermine, for the night is cold,
And wrap her warmly, for the night is long ;
In pious hands the flaming torches hold,
While her attendants, chosen from among

Her faithful virgin throng,
May lay her in her cedar litter,
Decking her coverlet with sprigs of gold,
Roses, and lilies white that best befit her.

Sound flute and tabor, that the bridal be
Not without music, nor with these alone ;
But let the viol lead the melody,
With lesser intervals, and plaintive moan
Of sinking semitone ;
And, all in choir, the virgin voices
Rest not from singing in skilled harmony
The song that aye the bridegroom's ear rejoices.

Let the priests go before, arrayed in white,
And let the dark-stoled minstrels follow slow,
Next they that bear her, honoured on this night,
And then the maidens, in a double row,
Each singing soft and low,
And each on high a torch upstaying :
Unto her lover lead her forth with light,
With music, and with singing, and with praying.

'Twas at this sheltering hour he nightly came,
And found her trusty window open wide,
And knew the signal of the timorous flame,
That long the restless curtain would not hide
Her form that stood beside ;
As scarce she dared to be delighted,
Listening to that sweet tale, that is no shame
To faithful lovers, that their hearts have plighted.

But now for many days the dewy grass
Has shown no markings of his feet at morn :
And watching she has seen no shadow pass
The moonlit walk, and heard no music borne
    Upon her ear forlorn.
   In vain she has looked out to greet him ;
  He has not come, he will not come, alas !
So let us bear her out where she must meet him.

Now to the river bank the priests are come :
The bark is ready to receive its freight :
Let some prepare her place therein, and some
Embark the litter with its slender weight :
    The rest stand by in state,
    And sing her a safe passage over ;
  While she is oared across to her new home,
Into the arms of her expectant lover.

And thou, O lover, that art on the watch,
Where, on the banks of the forgetful streams,
The pale indifferent ghosts wander, and snatch
The sweeter moments of their broken dreams,—
    Thou, when the torchlight gleams,
   When thou shalt see the slow procession,
  And when thine ears the fitful music catch,
Rejoice, for thou art near to thy possession.
                Robert Bridges.

142. AN EPITAPH

HERE lies a most beautiful lady,
   Light of step and heart was she ;
I think she was the most beautiful lady
That ever was in the West Country.
But beauty vanishes ; beauty passes ;
However rare—rare it be ;
And when I crumble, who will remember
This lady of the West Country ?

Walter de la Mare.

143. A DREAM OF DEATH

I DREAMED that one had died in a strange place
   Near no accustomed hand ;
And they had nailed the boards above her face,
The peasants of that land,
And, wondering, planted by her solitude
A cypress and a yew :
I came, and wrote upon a cross of wood,
Man had no more to do :
She was more beautiful than thy first love,
This lady by the trees :
And gazed upon the mournful stars above,
And heard the mournful breeze.

W. B. Yeats.

144. A DREAM OF A BLESSED SPIRIT

ALL the heavy days are over ;
   Leave the body's coloured pride
Underneath the grass and clover,
With the feet laid side by side.

One with her are mirth and duty;
Bear the gold embroidered dress,
For she needs not her sad beauty,
To the scented oaken press.

Hers the kiss of Mother Mary,
The long hair is on her face ;
Still she goes with footsteps wary,
Full of earth's old timid grace:

With white feet of angels seven
Her white feet go glimmering ;
And above the deep of heaven,
Flame on flame and wing on wing.

W. B. Yeats.

145. MESSAGES

WHAT shall I your true-love tell,
    Earth-forsaking maid ?
What shall I your true-love tell,
    When life's spectre's laid ?

" Tell him that, our side the grave,
    Maid may not conceive
Life should be so sad to have,
    That's so sad to leave ! "

What shall I your true-love tell,
    When I come to him ?
What shall I your true-love tell—
    Eyes growing dim !

" Tell him this, when you shall part
    From a maiden pined ;
That I see him with my heart,
    Now my eyes are blind."

What shall I your true-love tell ?
    Speaking-while is scant.
What shall I your true-love tell,
    Death's white postulant ?

" Tell him—love, with speech at strife,
    For last utterance saith :
I, who loved with all my life,
    Love with all my death."

Francis Thompson.

146. THE FOLLY OF BEING COMFORTED

ONE that is ever kind said yesterday :
    " Your well-beloved's hair has threads of grey,
And little shadows come about her eyes ;
Time can but make it easier to be wise,
Though now it's hard, till trouble is at an end ;
And so be patient, be wise and patient, friend."
But, heart, there is no comfort, not a grain ;
Time can but make her beauty over again,
Because of that great nobleness of hers ;
The fire that stirs about her, when she stirs
Burns but more clearly.   O she had not these ways,
When all the wild summer was in her gaze.
O heart ! O heart ! if she'd but turn her head,
You'd know the folly of being comforted.

W. B. Yeats.

147. AT NIGHT

To W. M

HOME, home from the horizon far and clear,
  Hither the soft wings sweep ;
Flocks of the memories of the day draw near
  The dovecote doors of sleep.

Oh, which are they that come through sweetest light
  Of all these homing birds ?
Which with the straightest and the swiftest flight ?
  Your words to me, your words !

Alice Meynell.

INDEX OF FIRST LINES

171

SIDGWICK & JACKSON'S BOOKS FOR SCHOOLS

GREAT SCHOOLS OF PAINTING. A First Book of European Art. By WINIFRED TURNER. With 32 Plates. 5s. net.

"A study which should be exceedingly acceptable to conductors of art classes for the young."—*Pall Mall Gazette.*

GREAT SCHOOLS OF SCULPTURE. By WINIFRED TURNER. With 48 Plates. 5s. net. [*In preparation.*

BRITISH PAINTING. A First Book for Students. By IRENE MAGUINNESS. With 48 Plates. 5s. net.
[*In preparation.*

THE ROMANCE OF LANGUAGE. By M. A. CHAPLIN. With Illustrations. 5s. net. [*In preparation.*

HOW TO TEACH NATURE STUDY. By T. W. HOARE. Profusely Illustrated. New and cheaper edition. 2s. 6d. net.

"Mr. Hoare has provided in his book a regular course through which any energetic man or woman could take a class of children with little in the way of expense."—*Spectator.*

HOUSEHOLD FOES. A First Book of Health and Hygiene for Boys and Girls. By ALICE RAVENHILL. With 100 Illustrations. 2s. 6d.

"For simplicity of treatment we have seen no book to surpass the one before us. It is sufficiently bright and interesting for a class reader in either elementary or secondary schools."—*Journal of Education.*

STORIES FROM OLD CHRONICLES. Edited with Introductions by KATE STEPHENS. 1s. 6d.

** On the London County Council's requisition list.

"These early Chronicles should be welcomed by those who care for the actual and legendary history of their own country 'as heard out of the mouths of the men who did and saw.'"—*Education.*

SIDGWICK & JACKSON'S POETRY AND DRAMA

Rupert Brooke
POEMS. 2s. 6d. net. *Eighth Impression.*
1914 AND OTHER POEMS. 2s. 6d. net.
[*Ninth Impression.*

John Drinkwater
SWORDS AND PLOUGHSHARES. 2s. 6d. net.

Gerald Gould
POEMS. 1s. 6d. net. *Second Impression.*
MY LADY'S BOOK. 2s. 6d. net.

Laurence Housman
SELECTED POEMS. 3s. 6d. net.

Rose Macaulay
THE TWO BLIND COUNTRIES. 2s. 6d. net.

Katharine Tynan
INNOCENCIES.
NEW POEMS. *Second Impression.*
IRISH POEMS.
FLOWER OF YOUTH : Poems in War-Time.
Each, 3s. 6d. net.

THE WILD HARP : A Selection from Irish Poetry. By
KATHARINE TYNAN. Decorated. 7s. 6d. net.

PRUNELLA : or Love in a Dutch Garden. A Play
by LAURENCE HOUSMAN and GRANVILLE BARKER.
Library Edition, 5s. net. Also Crown 8vo, paper
wrappers, 1s. net. [*Ninth Impression.*

FOUR PLAYS FOR CHILDREN. By ETHEL SIDG-
WICK. 2s. net. [*Second Impression.*
(Thackeray's Rose and the Ring, The Goody-Witch, The Goose
Girl, and Boots and the North Wind.)

CINDERELLA. A Play for Children, with Songs. By
E. NESBIT. Paper. 6d. net.

SIDGWICK & JACKSON, Ltd., 3 Adam Street, London, W.C.